פרקי אבת

Pirkei Avot

Ethics of the Fathers

WITH A NEW COMMENTARY ANTHOLOGIZED FROM
THE WORKS OF THE CLASSIC COMMENTATORS
AND THE CHASIDIC MASTERS

Compiled by

Rabbi Yosef Marcus

PUBLISHED AND COPYRIGHTED BY
MERKOS L'INYONEI CHINUCH
770 EASTERN PARKWAY • BROOKLYN, NEW YORK 11213
5765 • 2005

PIRKEI AVOT
ETHICS OF THE FATHERS

Published and Copyrighted © 2005
by
MERKOS L'INYONEI CHINUCH
770 Eastern Parkway / Brooklyn, New York 11213
(718) 774-4000 / Fax (718) 774-2718

Orders:
291 Kingston Avenue / Brooklyn, New York 11213
(718) 778-0226 / Fax (718) 778-4148
www.kehotonline.com

ISBN 0-8266-0147-2

Manufactured in the United States of America

CONTENTS

PREFACE

It is with gratitude to the Almighty that we present this new edition of *Pirkei Avot: Ethics of the Fathers*, with a collection of selected commentaries anthologized from the works of the classic commentators and the Chasidic Masters.

The anthology of commentaries in this volume was compiled by Rabbi Yosef Marcus. The translation of the Mishnayot is based on Rabbi Nissan Mangel's translation (published in *Siddur Tehillat Hashem* (Merkos, 1978)) and was in some instances modified by Rabbi Marcus.

The project was directed by Rabbi Yosef B. Friedman. Special thanks are due Rabbis Dovid Olidort, Avraham Vaisfiche, Ari Sollish and Shmuel Marcus.

Merkos L'Inyonei Chinuch

11 Nissan 5765

INTRODUCTION

INTRODUCTION

> He who wishes to become a *chasid*
> should fulfill the words of *Avot*.
> —*Bava Kama* 30a

Fifty-nine of the sixty tractates of the Mishnah—the corpus of Jewish law edited by Rabbi Yehudah the Prince in the 2nd century C.E.—instruct on how to fulfill the requirements of the Torah: what time to pray each day, how to keep the Shabbat, and so on. Follow all the laws set out in these fifty-nine tractates and you are a *tzaddik*, a righteous human being.

The Tractate of Avot, in contrast, speaks to the aspiring *chasid*, one who seeks to go beyond the letter of the law.

While the rest of Mishnah deals primarily with the pragmatic details of ritual and regulation, Avot speaks to the person beneath and behind the actions—to one's character. In Avot one will not find an instruction to honor others or to protect their property—that is a given. Avot demands that the property and honor of others should be as dear to you *as your own*; that not only should you do a mitzvah, you should *run* to do a mitzvah; not only should you give charity, you should *want* to give charity.

WHAT IS A CHASID?

Long before the 18th century, when Rabbi Israel Baal Shem Tov founded the Chasidic movement, the term *chasid* was used in the Talmud to refer to a humble and altruistic person who went beyond the letter of the law in observance of Torah.

The word *chasid* is derived from the word *chesed*, kindness. The chasid is both kind to his fellow and, according to the *Zohar*, seeks to do kindness to G-d. "He is like a son who exerts himself for his father and mother, whom he loves more than himself. He would sacrifice his life for their sake, to redeem them would they be held in captivity." Similarly, the chasid is motivated solely by the desire to serve G-d and re-

deem and reveal His presence, which is held "captive" in this world (*Tanya*, chapter 10 citing *Ra'aya Mehemna, Tetze*).

A chasid spends nine hours a day in prayer (*Brachot* 32b), rejoices with the chance to do a mitzvah (*Tosefta, Peah* 2) and accepts the strictest form of Torah observance (see *Shabbat*

THE CHASID IN THE TALMUD

• The early chasidim would go to the house of a mourner before attending a house of celebration (*Smachot* 12:5).

• The early chasidim would meditate for one hour, pray for one hour, and meditate again for an hour after praying. If they spent nine hours a day in prayer [since each of the three daily prayers took them three hours], how could their Torah study have been kept and how could their work have been done? Because they were chasidim, their Torah was kept and their work was done (*Brachot* 32b).

• [During the Sukkot celebration in the Temple] chasidim and men of deeds would dance while juggling torches... (*Sukkah* 51a).

• Chasidut brings one to humility... Chasidut brings one to Divine inspiration (*Kallah* 2).

• Chasidim are different because they are strict with themselves (*Menachot* 41a).

• A chasid once discovered a gap in his fence on Shabbat and planned on repairing it. Realizing that he thought these thoughts on Shabbat, he did not want to follow up on his plan, and decided never to make the repair. A miracle was done for him and a large tree grew in that spot, which provided him and his family with a livelihood (*Shabbat* 150b).

• A chasid was once praying on the road when he was greeted by a nobleman. The chasid chose not to interrupt his prayers and the nobleman waited until he was finished, whereupon the nobleman shouted at him: "Doesn't your Torah command you to protect your life? I could have beheaded you for offending me!" To which the chasid replied: "If you were standing before a mortal king and someone greeted you, would you respond? Of course not. And if you would respond, you would be executed. While praying, I am standing before the eternal King of Kings. Surely you would not expect me to return your greeting" (*Brachot* 32b).

• A chasid once forgot a sheaf in the field. [It is a mitzvah to leave forgotten sheaves in the field for the poor.] The chasid was so happy that he told his son to offer two sacrifices in celebration. When his son asked, "Why do you rejoice over this mitzvah more than any other?" the chasid replied: "G-d gave us all other *mitzvot* to be done knowingly; this is the only one that must be done unknowingly" (*Tosefta, Pe'ah* 2).

150b; *Rambam, Hilchot De'ot* 1:9). The chasid is willing to cause harm to himself so that his fellow will not be harmed (*Tosfot, Niddah* s.v. *sorfan chasid* 17a).

The chasid is an egoless servant of G-d, whose Divine soul dominates his spirit and deed.

And *Avot* is the chasid's manual.

COMMENTARY

To be sure, several of Avot's sayings do not seem to address the aspiring chasid. Avot speaks also to one struggling to live a G-dly and pure life: "Consider the gain of a sin opposite the loss it incurs" (2:1); "Envy, lust and honor drive a person from the world." (4:21) Avot reminds its reader that his beginning is a putrid drop and his end is worms (3:1). One Mishnah even talks about the sins of idolatry and murder (5:9). Additionally, Avot is customarily studied during the summer months to counter the pleasure-seeking climate of the summer. Certainly, then, Avot is a book for every person, even one far beneath the level of a chasid.

Nevertheless, every statement in Avot can be read as an instruction to the aspiring chasid as well, which every person can ultimately be (see commentary on "All of Israel").

The Mishnah lends itself to numerous interpretations. Beneath the straightforward meaning, apparent even from a cursory reading, lie deeper meanings and allusions hinted to in

---

AVOT: THE NAME

• The Talmud (*Bava Kama* 30a) refers to this tractate as *the words of the fathers*, referring to the "fathers," our sages, who spoke these words.

But the name *Avot*, Fathers, refers also to the sayings themselves. For the moral teachings of *Avot* are the principles that fashion the character of a true student of Torah. (The other tractates of the Mishnah teach specific issues within Torah law.) It is therefore called *Avot*, Fathers, since the sayings it contains are the "fathers," the principles upon which all study and fulfillment of Torah must be based (*Biurim* intro.; cf. *Tiferet Yisrael*). Avot is a general tractate that sheds light on the rest of the Mishnah.

This explains a certain commonality between the Mishnah as a whole and tractate Avot: The Mishna begins with the letter *Mem* and ends with the letter *Mem*; the same is true of *Avot* (*Biurim*).

the choice of one word over another, the unique construct of a phrase, the author of the saying, the juxtaposition of the passages, the placement of seemingly unrelated maxims within one passage, and other nuances.

So even if on the straightforward level the Mishnah is talking about actual idolatry—to which the aspiring chasid has no connection—on a deeper level, the notion of idolatry, of worshipping something other than the one G-d, can be a metaphor for the self-worship of arrogance or anger. As our Sages say: "One who grows angry is as if he worships idols" (*Zohar* I:27b; III:179a; *Rambam, Hilchot De'ot* 2:3 in the name of the "early sages").

(And this is not mere hyperbole. As the founder of Chabad Chasidism, Rabbi Schneur Zalman of Liadi, explains, one who is upset about an event is essentially saying that G-d did not cause that event to happen, G-d forbid. For if he believed that it was G-d's doing he would not be upset, since surely all that G-d does is for the good. His anger exposes his assumption that the event occurred without G-d's involvement, G-d forbid. That is, to a certain extent, idolatry.)

Another example: The Mishnah states that one should pray for the welfare of the kingdom, since if not for the fear of it, "man would swallow his fellow alive" (3:2). The notion that men would destroy each other if not for the fear of the authorities does not seem to have any bearing on the chasid's world. But a deeper look into the Mishnah reveals that it is also an instruction to pray for the welfare of the kingdom of *Heaven* (*Ritva*) and that swallowing one's fellow alive refers to a failure to recognize one's fellow's worth. One who is lacking

---

AVOT: THE NAME (*continued*)

• The teachings of Avot refine a person's character. Since one who guides another person and leads him on the path of self-actualization is considered to have fathered him, the sages of this tractate are therefore called "fathers" (*Tosfot Yom Tov; Midrash Shmuel*).

• This is a tractate that every father must study and internalize so that he will know how to guide his children toward refined character, purity and love of Torah (*Meam Loez*).

in the humbling sense of awe for the kingdom of Heaven is liable to treat others as accessories to his needs—he "swallows them alive," denying them their own identity.

This interpretation does not detract from or contradict the plain meaning of the Mishnah, which is advocating government—even an imperfect one—over anarchy. Each interpretation, if true to the codes and methodology of Torah study, is a part of Torah and contained within the words of the Mishnah.

THIS COMMENTARY

Hundreds of commentaries have been written on Pirkei Avot, each one highlighting another shade of meaning in the text, and brought to light by the unique souls of the individual commentators.

The purpose of the present commentary is to explain the obscure and illuminate the plain—all in about 100 pages, half of which is taken up by the Mishnah text proper.

More precisely, our first purpose is to explain any saying or concept whose meaning is not obvious to the average reader. The commentary therefore becomes heavier as the tractate wears on because of the more complex nature of the later chapters. Secondly, where the straightforward meaning of the text may leave the reader unsatisfied, the commentary offers a deeper dimension or explanation to the passage.

The commentary also aims to provide a broader meaning to dictums whose simple meaning seems to address a narrow audience, such as the instruction to the judge: "Interrogate witnesses extensively" (1:9).

Additionally, an effort is made to demonstrate the preciseness and significance of each word of the Mishnah, including the words, details and seeming redundancies that may appear arbitrary from a cursory reading. So, while not every word and nuance is accounted for, a number of instances were chosen to serve as examples for the rest (see, for example, 6:7).

A particular emphasis is placed on including interpretations that convey ideas emphasized in Chasidic phi-

losophy in general and Chabad philosophy in particular, especially in the philosophy of the Lubavitcher Rebbe, Rabbi Menachem M. Schneerson, of blessed memory.

Finally, the compiler included comments that seemed particularly interesting or insightful.

THE SOURCES

The present commentary does not consist of original insights. It is a compilation of comments made by earlier commentators.

The bulk of the commentary derives from the talks of the Lubavitcher Rebbe, whose comments on Avot could fill several volumes. These were compiled and condensed by Rabbi Eli Friedman of Safed, Israel, and published under the title *Biurim L'pirkei Avot*—Explanations to Pirkei Avot (Kehot, 1996). This work is referred to as *Biurim* throughout the commentary.

At times the Rebbe's commentary is based on or similar to those of earlier commentators. When we have discovered an earlier source, both the earlier source and *Biurim*, where the idea is often embellished, are cited. (Whenever a comment of the Rebbe is cited from a source other than *Biurim*, such as *Likkutei Sichot* (the 39-volume collection of the Rebbe's edited talks), the exact source is cited.)

The second most oft-quoted sources are *Derech Chaim* and *Midrash Shmuel*. *Derech Chaim*, published in Krakow in 1589, is a philosophic/mystic interpretation of Avot by the famed Rabbi Yehudah Loewe of Prague, popularly known as the Maharal. *Midrash Shmuel*, published in Venice in 1579 and arguably the most popular commentary on Avot to this day, is an anthology of earlier commentaries—including Abarbanel, Rabbi Moshe Almoshnino, Hachasid Yaavetz, Rabbi Moshe Alashkar, and others—as well as original interpretation by Rabbi Shmuel de Ozido, a student of the famed Kabbalist R. Yitzchak Luria, commonly known as the Arizal.

Others sources include the early commentators such as *Rashi, Rambam, Meiri, Bartenura, Sforno,* as well as later commentators including *Chida, Tiferet Yisrael,* the Chasidic Mas-

ters and others. See the bibliography for a complete listing of all sources cited.

It should be noted that often the same interpretation is offered by a number of commentators. In these instances, not all of the sources have been cited; often *Bartenura*, will be cited for example, even if the same interpretation is offered by an earlier commentator, such as *Rambam*.

Important Note on the Commentary: Each comment is only one interpretation out of the many that have been offered. "Longer than the earth is the Torah's measure, and wider than the sea…" (Job 11:9). Often, the commentary will make no mention of the plain or straightforward meaning of the Mishnah at all and offer a more metaphoric or esoteric interpretation. These are not meant to negate the plain meaning but rather to offer something in addition to it. Also, not always was an effort made to provide a singular approach to a given Mishnah. At times, therefore, the interpretation given on one phrase may differ or even (seemingly) negate an interpretation offered on another phrase in the very same Mishnah.

*   *   *

It is hoped that this volume will contribute to the appreciation of the wisdom of Pirkei Avot and its application to daily life. May this increase in wisdom help usher in the day when "the land will be filled with the knowledge of G-d as the water covers the sea" (Isaiah 11:9).

Yosef Marcus
S. Mateo, California

PIRKEI AVOT

• THE CUSTOM OF READING AVOT DURING THE SUMMER

The following customs are cited in the siddur edited by
R. Schneur Zalman of Liadi:

It is customary to say one chapter of *Pirkei Avot* on each of the Sabbaths between Passover and Shavuot in the afternoon.

Before beginning each chapter, say the Mishnah *"All of Israel...."* After concluding each chapter, say the Mishnah *"R. Chananyah ben Akashya...."*

Some continue to observe this custom throughout all the summer Sabbaths.

It is customary to say one chapter. The earliest record of this custom is the 9th century *Siddur Rav Amram Gaon*.

To say one chapter. Although the custom is to *say* the chapters, rather than study them, one should study at least one *Mishnah* or a few *Mishnayot* in depth each week (*Biurim*).

Between Passover and Shavuot. One thereby completes the six chapters over the six-week period between Passover and Shavuot.

This is the period of "the counting of the *omer*," a time for introspection and refinement of one's character in preparation for the giving of the To-rah.

The study and application of the moral teachings of Avot serves as a preparation for receiving the Torah on Shavuot. For "the Torah will only dwell in one free of negative traits and filled with virtues" (*Midrash Shmuel*; *Biurim*).

Shabbat afternoon. Customarily, the chapter is read after the Minchah prayer. The late afternoon of Shabbat is considered the loftiest and holiest time of Shabbat and is therefore an auspicious time for the recitation of *Pirkei Avot* (see *Maharal*, intro.).

Throughout the summer. I.e., until Rosh Hashanah. During the last few weeks of the summer, it is sometimes necessary to recite two chapters on one Shabbat, so as to complete the tractate before Rosh Hashanah.

The summer climate can lead a person toward indulgence in the physical, and distraction from spiritual practice. The study of Avot is meant to redirect one's focus toward higher ideals (*Midrash Shmuel*).

כָּל יִשְׂרָאֵל

כָּל יִשְׂרָאֵל יֵשׁ לָהֶם חֵלֶק לְעוֹלָם הַבָּא, שֶׁנֶּאֱמַר:
וְעַמֵּךְ כֻּלָּם צַדִּיקִים, לְעוֹלָם יִירְשׁוּ אָרֶץ, נֵצֶר מַטָּעַי
מַעֲשֵׂה יָדַי לְהִתְפָּאֵר.

---

to Paradise, where souls that have passed on delight in Divine splendor. For not every soul merits this revelation (*Likkutei Sichot*, 17:344; see, however, *Rambam*). Rather, this refers to the Messianic Era, when every soul that has ever lived will return to the physical world and be clothed in a body, enjoying the fulfillment of G-d's ultimate plan: the creation of a Divine dwelling in the physical world (see *Bartenura, Midrash Shmuel*).

Even one who has committed capital crimes is admitted into the World to Come after receiving his punishment (*Rambam*).

Are all righteous, regardless of their fulfillment of *mitzvot* or lack thereof (*Maharal*).

Will inherit The Land of eternal life (*Maharal*).

Will inherit the Land forever. An inheritance does not require any action on the part of the inheritor. Similarly, all of Israel, by virtue of their very being, are inheritors of *the land forever*, i.e., the World to Come and eternal life. Nevertheless:

The branch of My planting. Just as a planting must be tended to in order to grow properly, the individual— despite his inherent share in the World to Come—must put forth his own effort in order to actualize his full potential (*Biurim*). Although every person has a share in the World to Come, the quality of that share is dependent upon one's actions (*Bartenura*).

4

ALL OF ISRAEL

All of Israel have a share in the World to Come, as it says, *Your people are all righteous; they will inherit the Land forever; they are the branch of My planting, the work of My hands in which I take pride.* (*Sanhedrin* 11:1)

All of Israel. This Mishnah is not part of Avot. It is a Mishnah from Tractate *Sanhedrin*, which is customarily recited prior to the recitation of Avot during the summer months.

The following are a few of the reasons given for the custom to read "All of Israel" before studying Avot:

❏ One might have thought that Avot, which demands that one go beyond the letter of the law, is not applicable to every person. We therefore begin our study of Avot with a Mishnah that praises *all* of Israel, insinuating that every Jew can and must fulfill the words of Avot (*Biurim*).

❏ It is because of his loftiness—as expressed in the passage *All of Israel*—that the Jew is capable of implementing the challenging teachings of Avot (*Maharal; Biurim*).

❏ Avot is read as a preparation to receive the Torah on the holiday of Shavuot. The first step in this preparation must be to engage in acts of love towards one's fellow. We therefore read *All of Israel*, which helps us appreciate the value and loftiness of our fellows and overcome our natural biases (*Biurim*).

The World to Come. The World to Come in this context does not refer

1. Isaiah 60:21.

פֶּרֶק רִאשׁוֹן

כָּל יִשְׂרָאֵל יֵשׁ לָהֶם חֵלֶק לְעוֹלָם הַבָּא, שֶׁנֶּאֱמַר: וְעַמֵּךְ כֻּלָּם צַדִּיקִים, לְעוֹלָם יִירְשׁוּ אָרֶץ, נֵצֶר מַטָּעַי מַעֲשֵׂה יָדַי לְהִתְפָּאֵר.

א. מֹשֶׁה קִבֵּל תּוֹרָה מִסִּינַי וּמְסָרָהּ לִיהוֹשֻׁעַ, וִיהוֹשֻׁעַ לִזְקֵנִים, וּזְקֵנִים לִנְבִיאִים, וּנְבִיאִים מְסָרוּהָ לְאַנְשֵׁי כְנֶסֶת הַגְּדוֹלָה. הֵם אָמְרוּ שְׁלֹשָׁה דְבָרִים: הֱווּ מְתוּנִים בַּדִּין, וְהַעֲמִידוּ תַלְמִידִים הַרְבֵּה, וַעֲשׂוּ סְיָג לַתּוֹרָה.

ב. שִׁמְעוֹן הַצַּדִּיק הָיָה מִשְּׁיָרֵי כְנֶסֶת הַגְּדוֹלָה. הוּא הָיָה אוֹמֵר, עַל

Elders. After Yehoshua's passing, the era of the Elders began with Otniel ben Knaz and continued for some three centuries through the era of the Judges, ending with Eli the High Priest (*Meiri; Magen Avot*).

Prophets. The era of the Prophets lasted for some six centuries, beginning with Shmuel and ending with the passing of Chaggai, Zechariah, and Malachi.

The Great Assembly. A council of 120 elders and prophets headed by Ezra the Scribe that functioned for about 30 years (391—361 B.C.E.). These sages faced the challenge of rebuilding and fortifying Judaism after the upheaval and assimilation caused by the Babylonian exile. They fixed the Biblical canon, introduced daily prayer and its liturgy, *Kiddush*, *Havdalah*, and many other practices that have shaped Jewish practice to this day.

● They were called the "great" assembly because they restored G-d's greatness in the eyes of the people even amid the persecution of His children and the destruction of His Temple (*Bartenura*, from *Yoma* 69b).

They said three things. These three dictums are their formula for perpetuating the Torah (*Bartenura*) in a spiritually deteriorating world (see *Maharal*).

Be patient in judgment. A judge should consider a case carefully before ruling (*Mefarshim*). Also, be patient in judging others for their poor Jewish observance. Recognize the cause for this condition, which is Exile. By judging them favorably and seeing that despite the Exile there is so much they do observe, one will pursue many potential students, even those who to others seem "lost" (*Biurim*).

Make a fence around the Torah. Create the environment and conditions in which the Torah's ideals can be optimally realized (*Mefarshim*). In each generation, apply the Torah to the specific conditions of the time while remaining true to the principles received by Moshe at Sinai (*Biurim*).

CHAPTER ONE

All of Israel have a share in the World to Come, as it says, *Your people are all righteous; they will inherit the Land forever; they are the branch of My planting, the work of My hands in which I take pride.*[1] (*Sanhedrin* 11:1)

———————

1. Moshe received the Torah from Sinai and passed it on to Yehoshua; Yehoshua to the Elders; the Elders to the Prophets; and the Prophets passed it on to the Men of the Great Assembly. They said three things: Be patient in judgment; raise many disciples; and make a fence around the Torah.

2. Shimon the Tzaddik was from the last of the Men of the Great

———————

1. Moshe received. Avot contains the principles by which the Torah can be received and passed on throughout the generations. It therefore begins with a history of the transmission of Torah (see *Midrash Shmuel*).

Additionally, this preface indicates that the teachings of Avot are not just the personal reflections of the Sages—they are part of a tradition that harks back to the Divine revelation at Sinai (*Bartenura*; see *Sfat Emet*).

The Torah. This refers to Scripture and its interpretation. The latter was passed down orally from generation to generation until it was partially transcribed by R. Yehudah the Prince (2nd century) and more so in the Talmud (5th century) (see *R. Yonah*).

From Sinai. From the One who revealed Himself at Sinai (*Bartenura*). G-d is not referred to directly, since it would be inappropriate to include the Creator in the list of human beings mentioned in the Mishnah (*Maharal*).

Yehoshua. Although Moshe taught Torah to the *entire* nation (*Eiruvin* 54b), Yehoshua was the one individual of his generation chosen to be *the* recipient and transmitter of Torah, especially the Oral Torah, to the next generation (*Mefarshim*).

LEADER(S)	ERA (B.C.E.)
Moshe	1313–1273
Joshua	1273–1245
Elders	1245–931
Prophets	931–313*
Great Assembly	c. 391–361
(Mishnah)	(188 C.E.)

———————

* Prophecy continued to exist—even after the establishment of the Great Assembly—until 313 B.C.E. (or 307 according to others). see Kaplan, *Handbook of Jewish Thought*, vol. 1, p. 111.

———————

1. Isaiah 60:21.

שְׁלשָׁה דְבָרִים הָעוֹלָם עוֹמֵד: עַל הַתּוֹרָה, וְעַל הָעֲבוֹדָה, וְעַל גְּמִילוּת חֲסָדִים.

ג. אַנְטִיגְנוֹס אִישׁ סוֹכוֹ קִבֵּל מִשִּׁמְעוֹן הַצַּדִּיק. הוּא הָיָה אוֹמֵר: אַל תִּהְיוּ כַּעֲבָדִים הַמְשַׁמְּשִׁין אֶת הָרַב עַל מְנָת לְקַבֵּל פְּרָס, אֶלָּא הֱווּ כַּעֲבָדִים הַמְשַׁמְּשִׁין אֶת הָרַב שֶׁלֹּא עַל מְנָת לְקַבֵּל פְּרָס, וִיהִי מוֹרָא שָׁמַיִם עֲלֵיכֶם.

ד. יוֹסֵי בֶּן יוֹעֶזֶר אִישׁ צְרֵדָה וְיוֹסֵי בֶּן יוֹחָנָן אִישׁ יְרוּשָׁלַיִם קִבְּלוּ מֵהֶם. יוֹסֵי בֶּן יוֹעֶזֶר אִישׁ צְרֵדָה אוֹמֵר: יְהִי בֵיתְךָ בֵּית וַעַד לַחֲכָמִים, וֶהֱוֵי מִתְאַבֵּק בַּעֲפַר רַגְלֵיהֶם, וֶהֱוֵי שׁוֹתֶה בַצָּמָא אֶת דִּבְרֵיהֶם.

ה. יוֹסֵי בֶּן יוֹחָנָן אִישׁ יְרוּשָׁלַיִם אוֹמֵר: יְהִי בֵיתְךָ פָּתוּחַ לִרְוָחָה, וְיִהְיוּ עֲנִיִּים בְּנֵי בֵיתֶךָ, וְאַל תַּרְבֶּה שִׂיחָה עִם הָאִשָּׁה, בְּאִשְׁתּוֹ אָמְרוּ, קַל וָחֹמֶר בְּאֵשֶׁת חֲבֵרוֹ. מִכָּאן אָמְרוּ חֲכָמִים: כָּל הַמַּרְבֶּה שִׂיחָה עִם הָאִשָּׁה, גּוֹרֵם רָעָה לְעַצְמוֹ, וּבוֹטֵל מִדִּבְרֵי תוֹרָה, וְסוֹפוֹ יוֹרֵשׁ גֵּיהִנָּם.

ו. יְהוֹשֻׁעַ בֶּן פְּרַחְיָה וְנִתַּאי הָאַרְבֵּלִי קִבְּלוּ מֵהֶם. יְהוֹשֻׁעַ בֶּן פְּרַחְיָה אוֹמֵר: עֲשֵׂה לְךָ רַב, וּקְנֵה לְךָ חָבֵר, וֶהֱוֵי דָן אֶת כָּל הָאָדָם לְכַף זְכוּת.

"head of the court" (*Mefarshim*).

5. Chatter. This obviously does not refer to valuable conversation between husband and wife that enhances their relationship, but to excessive and pointless chatter (see *Meiri*). This Mishnah and the previous one dictate the proper atmosphere for one's home. Let it be a place of scholarship, hospitality and moral purity (see *Maharal*).

6. A teacher...friend. "Learn from teachers, not from books" (*Kuzari* 2:72). Without a teacher and a friend,

a person does not recognize his own shortcomings (see *R. Yonah, Mili d'Chasiduta*).

Judge every person favorably. Look favorably upon *every* person, even one who is spiritually deficient. Recognize that his shortcomings are due to the enormity of his challenges and that he must possess enormous potential to have been challenged so severely. By recognizing the extent of his spiritual power, one brings that latent potential—his "merit"—to the surface, enabling him to ultimately triumph (*Biurim*).

8

Assembly. He would say: The world stands on three things: Torah, worship, and deeds of kindness.

3. Antignos man of Socho received [the oral tradition] from Shimon the Tzaddik. He would say: Do not be like the servants who
serve the master in order to receive reward. Rather, be like the
servants who serve the master not in order to receive reward; and
let the fear of Heaven be upon you.

4. Yosay ben [son of] Yoezer man of Tzreidah and Yosay ben Yochanan man of Jerusalem received from them. Yosay ben Yoezer
said: Let your house be a meeting-house for scholars; grow dusty
by the dirt of their feet; and drink their words with thirst.

5. Yosay ben Yochanan said: Let your house be open wide; and let
the poor be the members of your household; and do not engage
in excessive chatter with a woman. This was said about one's
own wife; it certainly applies to the wife of one's friend. From
here the sages derived: Anyone who engages in excessive chatter
with a woman, causes evil to himself, neglects Torah study, and
in the end will inherit *Gehinom* [Purgatory].

6. Yehoshuah ben Perachya and Nittai of Arabel received from
them. Yehoshuah ben Perachya said: Make for yourself a teacher;
acquire for yourself a friend; and judge every person favorably.

---

2. He would say. The meaning of "he would say" throughout the tractate is that this was a favorite saying of the given sage. This is also the meaning of "Rabbi so-and-so said" throughout the tractate (*Bartenura*).

Worship. I.e., the sacrificial offerings and prayer.
  The three "pillars"—corresponding to mind, heart, and deed—sustain the world at large as well as the miniature world of the individual (see *Mili d'Chasiduta*; cf. Rambam, *Tiferet Yisrael*).

3. Not…to receive reward. Although

one receives physical and spiritual rewards for serving the Creator, one should strive to do so out of love and awe, without care for reward (*Mefarshim*).

Man of Socho, meaning the leader of the Socho Jewish community (*Rambam*, intro. to Mishnah).

4. THE PAIRS. In the case of all five "pairs" of sages mentioned in this chapter, the first of the pair served as the *nassi*, the "president" of the Sanhedrin, while the second served as his assistant, with the title *av bet din*,

ז. נִתַּאי הָאַרְבֵּלִי אוֹמֵר: הַרְחֵק מִשָּׁכֵן רָע, וְאַל תִּתְחַבֵּר לָרָשָׁע, וְאַל תִּתְיָאֵשׁ מִן הַפּוּרְעָנוּת.

ח. יְהוּדָה בֶּן טַבַּאי וְשִׁמְעוֹן בֶּן שָׁטַח קִבְּלוּ מֵהֶם. יְהוּדָה בֶּן טַבַּאי אוֹמֵר: אַל תַּעַשׂ עַצְמְךָ כְּעוֹרְכֵי הַדַּיָּנִין, וּכְשֶׁיִּהְיוּ בַּעֲלֵי הַדִּין עוֹמְדִים לְפָנֶיךָ. יִהְיוּ בְעֵינֶיךָ כִּרְשָׁעִים, וּכְשֶׁנִּפְטָרִים מִלְפָנֶיךָ יִהְיוּ בְעֵינֶיךָ כְּזַכָּאִין, כְּשֶׁקִּבְּלוּ עֲלֵיהֶם אֶת הַדִּין.

ט. שִׁמְעוֹן בֶּן שָׁטַח אוֹמֵר: הֱוֵי מַרְבֶּה לַחֲקוֹר אֶת הָעֵדִים, וֶהֱוֵי זָהִיר בִּדְבָרֶיךָ, שֶׁמָּא מִתּוֹכָם יִלְמְדוּ לְשַׁקֵּר.

י. שְׁמַעְיָה וְאַבְטַלְיוֹן קִבְּלוּ מֵהֶם. שְׁמַעְיָה אוֹמֵר: אֱהוֹב אֶת הַמְּלָאכָה וּשְׂנָא אֶת הָרַבָּנוּת, וְאַל תִּתְוַדַּע לָרָשׁוּת.

יא. אַבְטַלְיוֹן אוֹמֵר: חֲכָמִים, הִזָּהֲרוּ בְדִבְרֵיכֶם, שֶׁמָּא תָחוּבוּ חוֹבַת

---

struction can refer to the arguments and facts that confront a person and testify regarding the virtue or evil of a given course of action. Interrogate these "witnesses" extensively until you are certain of the proper path (see *Sfat Emet, Notzer Chesed*).

Be cautious with your words. Give no hint of what it is they might say for their testimony to be accepted (*Ramah*).

10. Abhor power. "Do not don the crown on your own initiative" (*Avot d'Rabbi Nattan* 11:2).

If a person is motivated by an altruistic desire to *serve* the people—not to exalt himself—he should become a leader. But he should abhor the desire to lord over others (see *Midrash Shmuel, Biurim*).

Do not fraternize with government.

I.e., with the intention of gaining some leadership position, unless your intention is to help the community. But even then, the fraternization should be done begrudgingly, unenthusiastically. The leader must recognize that the very need for political connections is a temporary condition of the Exile, not something to luxuriate in or grow arrogant about (*Biurim*).

11. Be careful with your words. While speaking to the masses, make sure that your words cannot be distorted. For if your audience includes spiritually corrupt individuals, they will distort your words to support their beliefs in the eyes of your students, who will then drink of these evil waters and die a spiritual death, causing a desecration of G-d's Name (*Rambam*).

The above occurred to Antignos,

10

7. Nitai of Arabel said: Distance yourself from a bad neighbor; do not attach yourself to a wicked person; and do not despair of punishment.

8. Yehudah ben Tabbai and Shimon ben Shatach received from them. Yehudah ben Tabbai said: Do not act as a lawyer; and when the litigants stand before you, regard them both as guilty; but when they leave, having accepted the judgment, regard them both as guiltless.

9. Shimon ben Shatach said: Interrogate witnesses extensively; and be cautious with your words, lest through them they [the witnesses or the litigants] learn to speak falsehood.

10. Shemayah and Avtalyon received from them. Shemayah said: Love work; abhor power; and do not fraternize with the government.

11. Avtalyon said: Sages, be careful with your words; for you may in-

---

7. Do not attach yourself to a wicked person. Do not distance yourself from the wicked person—befriend him and embrace him with love. But do not *attach* yourself to his negative traits, which will cause you to become like him. Rather, attach yourself to his soul, which is entirely pure, and bring him to the path of holiness (see *Biurim*; see also *Midrash Shmuel*).

Do not despair of punishment. When you see the wicked prosper, do not attach yourself to them in order to ride the wave of their success. For their time may come suddenly and you will fall along with them (*R. Yonah*).

8. Do not act as a lawyer. A judge (or any other person) is not allowed to advise a litigant on how to manipulate the legal system to his advantage, which includes prompting and pre-

paring the litigant, even if the litigant is certainly in the right (*Mefarshim*). In a broader sense, do not seek to rationalize and justify your misdeeds like a lawyer who uses convoluted logic to exonerate a clearly guilty individual (*Chida, Petach Einayim*).

When the litigants stand before you, regard them both as guilty. Do not be biased toward either party: be suspicious of the claims of both (*Bartenura*).

When the litigants leave, regard them as guiltless. Even if one was clearly lying, assume that he does not have the money to pay and therefore denies the charges, intending to pay up when he has the means (*Me'am Loez*).

9. Interrogate witnesses. In addition to its obvious meaning, the in-

גָּלוּת וְתִגְלוּ לִמְקוֹם מַיִם הָרָעִים, וְיִשְׁתּוּ הַתַּלְמִידִים הַבָּאִים אַחֲרֵיכֶם וְיָמוּתוּ, וְנִמְצָא שֵׁם שָׁמַיִם מִתְחַלֵּל.

יב. הִלֵּל וְשַׁמַּאי קִבְּלוּ מֵהֶם. הִלֵּל אוֹמֵר: הֱוֵי מִתַּלְמִידָיו שֶׁל אַהֲרֹן, אוֹהֵב שָׁלוֹם וְרוֹדֵף שָׁלוֹם, אוֹהֵב אֶת הַבְּרִיּוֹת, וּמְקָרְבָן לַתּוֹרָה.

יג. הוּא הָיָה אוֹמֵר: נְגַד שְׁמָא אֲבַד שְׁמֵהּ, וּדְלָא מוֹסִיף יָסֵף, וּדְלָא יָלִיף קְטָלָא חַיָּב, וּדְאִשְׁתַּמֵּשׁ בְּתַגָּא חֲלָף.

יד. הוּא הָיָה אוֹמֵר: אִם אֵין אֲנִי לִי, מִי לִי, וּכְשֶׁאֲנִי לְעַצְמִי, מָה אֲנִי, וְאִם לֹא עַכְשָׁו, אֵימָתַי.

טו. שַׁמַּאי אוֹמֵר: עֲשֵׂה תוֹרָתְךָ קֶבַע, אֱמוֹר מְעַט וַעֲשֵׂה הַרְבֵּה, וֶהֱוֵי מְקַבֵּל אֶת כָּל הָאָדָם בְּסֵבֶר פָּנִים יָפוֹת.

טז. רַבָּן גַּמְלִיאֵל הָיָה אוֹמֵר: עֲשֵׂה לְךָ רַב, וְהִסְתַּלֵּק מִן הַסָּפֵק, וְאַל תַּרְבֶּה לְעַשֵּׂר אֲמָדוֹת.

---

13. He who does not teach deserves death. Although Hillel warns that one should not seek fame, one should also not refrain from teaching in an effort to remain humble. He who does not share his knowledge will ultimately lose it (*Biurim*).

14. If I am not for myself. A person must see himself as an important individual, whose unique potential and contribution to the world can only be actualized by his own efforts. But he must not forget that he is a part of the collective community, without which he cannot succeed (see *Mefarshim*).

If not now. If I do not change my character in my days of youth and strength, when will I—when I am old and feeble? (*Rambam*). Furthermore, if I do not seize this moment and fulfill its unique purpose, when can I retrieve it? (see *R.Y. ben Shushan*).

15. Make your Torah study a permanent thing. Make the study of Torah your primary pursuit; all else should be secondary (*Rambam*). If you can only study for a short period each day, make that study "permanent" —engraved upon your heart so that it lingers with you throughout the day (*Biurim*).

16. Provide yourself with a Teacher. Choose a rabbinic authority on whom to rely in the case of halachic questions. You will thereby remove yourself from halachic doubts (*Rambam*). Acquiring a teacher refers also to choosing a saintly master. When one is attached to a *tzaddik* all spiritual doubt and cynicism is silenced (*Knesset Yisrael* citing *Haflaah*).

Do not tithe by guesswork, even giving in excess. When a person tithes by estimate—even in excess of a tenth —he may at times give less than a

cur the penalty of exile and be banished to a place of evil waters [immoral views]; and the disciples who follow you there will drink and die, and consequently the Name of Heaven will be desecrated.

12. Hillel and Shammai received from them. Hillel said: Be of the disciples of Aharon: One who loves peace, pursues peace, loves his fellow creatures and draws them close to Torah.

13. He used to say: He who seeks to advance his name loses his name; he who does not increase [his knowledge of Torah] decreases it; he who does not teach deserves death; and he who makes use of the crown [of Torah for his own needs] will fade away.

14. He used to say: If I am not for myself, who will be for me? And if I am only for myself, what am I? And if not now, when?

15. Shamai said: Make your Torah study a permanent thing; speak little and do much; and receive every person with a pleasant face.

16. Rabban Gamliel said: Provide yourself with a teacher and free yourself of doubt; and do not tithe by guesswork, even giving in excess of the required amount.

---

who exhorted his generation to worship G-d without thought of reward (see above, Mishnah 3). His words were distorted by the Sadducees to support their denial of the concept of reward and punishment (*Rambam*).

12. Be of the disciples of Aharon. When Aharon knew of two quarrelling individuals, he would say to each one that the other party wished to make peace. When the two would meet, their quarrel would melt and they would embrace (*Avot d'Rabbi Nattan*).

Loves his fellow creatures. Aharon loved even those who were devoid of any merit, whose only redeeming fac-

tor was the fact that they were *creatures*, G-d's creations (see *Tanya* ch. 32). When Aharon befriended them, they would feel ashamed of their sins and would change their ways (*Avot d'Rabbi Nattan*).

Loves...draws them close to Torah. First of all, love the creature; then, bring him close to Torah. Love him for his soul's inherent loftiness, regardless of his actions.

Your love and acts of kindness should not be contingent upon your success in bringing him close to Torah. Yet if you truly love him you will seek also to unite him with the Torah, which will enable him to experience the inherent loftiness of his soul (*Biurim*).

13

יז. שִׁמְעוֹן בְּנוֹ אוֹמֵר: כָּל יָמַי גָּדַלְתִּי בֵּין הַחֲכָמִים, וְלֹא מָצָאתִי לַגּוּף טוֹב מִשְּׁתִיקָה, וְלֹא הַמִּדְרָשׁ עִקָּר אֶלָּא הַמַּעֲשֶׂה, וְכָל הַמַּרְבֶּה דְבָרִים מֵבִיא חֵטְא.

יח. רַבָּן שִׁמְעוֹן בֶּן גַּמְלִיאֵל אוֹמֵר, עַל שְׁלֹשָׁה דְבָרִים הָעוֹלָם קַיָּם: עַל הַדִּין, וְעַל הָאֱמֶת, וְעַל הַשָּׁלוֹם, שֶׁנֶּאֱמַר: אֱמֶת וּמִשְׁפַּט שָׁלוֹם שִׁפְטוּ בְּשַׁעֲרֵיכֶם.

רַבִּי חֲנַנְיָא בֶּן עֲקַשְׁיָא אוֹמֵר: רָצָה הַקָּדוֹשׁ בָּרוּךְ הוּא לְזַכּוֹת אֶת יִשְׂרָאֵל, לְפִיכָךְ הִרְבָּה לָהֶם תּוֹרָה וּמִצְוֹת, שֶׁנֶּאֱמַר: יְיָ חָפֵץ לְמַעַן צִדְקוֹ, יַגְדִּיל תּוֹרָה וְיַאְדִּיר.

Rabbi Chananya ben Akashya. This Mishnah is not part of Avot. It is a Mishnah from Tractate *Makkot* and is customarily recited after studying Torah with a group.

● When a quorum of ten study Torah together, the Kaddish prayer is customarily said afterward. However, the Kaddish should only be recited after reading a homiletic teaching (i.e., one that interprets a biblical verse— *Shulchan Aruch Harav, Orach Chaim* 54:4), since the world is sustained by the Kaddish recited after the study of homiletics (*Sotah* 49a).

It therefore became customary to conclude every session of study with this homiletic Mishnah from Tractate *Makkot* because of its beautiful ending (*Rashi*).

In abundance. When a person fulfills a mitzvah out of pure love of G-d, without any self-oriented motivation, he merits life in the World to Come. G-d therefore gave an abundance of commandments so that it would be impossible for a person to go through his entire life without fulfilling at least *one* mitzvah perfectly. And with that one mitzvah he acquires life for his soul (*Rambam*).

That one mitzvah serves as the channel through which the light of all the *mitzvot* shines upon him (*Likkutei Sichot*, 17:410, fn. 17).

[See additional commentary on this Mishnah at the conclusion of Chapter Six.]

17. Shimon his son said: All my days I grew up among the Sages and did not find anything better for the body than silence; not study but deed is the essential thing; and whoever engages in excessive talk brings on sin.

18. Rabban Shimon ben Gamliel said: The world endures by virtue of three things: justice, truth, and peace, as it says: *Administer truth and the justice of peace in your gates.*[2]

Rabbi Chananyah ben Akashya said: The Holy One, blessed be He, wished to make Israel meritorious. He therefore increased for them Torah and *mitzvot*, as it says: *G-d desired, for the sake of his [Israel's] righteousness, to make the Torah great and glorious.*[3] (*Makkot* 3:16)

tenth. Consistency is better than giving excessively on one occasion and deficiently on another (see *HaChasid*).

17. Anything better for the body than silence...deed is essential... excessive talk brings on sin. Silence, humility, and reclusive study is good for the person himself, but the purpose of creation is fulfilled through actual deed, not study. In fact, the purpose of study is that it guide and inspire one's deeds. Nevertheless, one should not be too aggressive in emerging from the world of silence and study, since *excessive* talk and involvement in the physical brings on misdeed (*Biurim*).

Excessive talk brings on sin. An abundance of words will inevitably contain something improper, such as gossip, etc. (*Rambam*).

18. The world endures by virtue of three things. The existence of the *world* is sustained by Torah, worship and deeds of kindness (above, Mishnah 2). But the world's *society*—"*your gates*" (*Biurim*)—is sustained by justice, truth and peace (*Meiri, Bartenura*).

Justice of peace. Through finding a compromise between the litigants, the judge can ensure that they will leave his court in peace (*Bayit L'Avot*).

---

2. Zechariah 8:16.   3. Isaiah 42:21.

פֶּרֶק שֵׁנִי

כָּל יִשְׂרָאֵל יֵשׁ לָהֶם חֵלֶק לְעוֹלָם הַבָּא, שֶׁנֶּאֱמַר: וְעַמֵּךְ כֻּלָּם צַדִּיקִים, לְעוֹלָם יִירְשׁוּ אָרֶץ, נֵצֶר מַטָּעַי מַעֲשֵׂה יָדַי לְהִתְפָּאֵר.

א. רַבִּי אוֹמֵר: אֵיזוֹ הִיא דֶרֶךְ יְשָׁרָה שֶׁיָּבוֹר לוֹ הָאָדָם, כָּל שֶׁהִיא תִפְאֶרֶת לְעֹשֶׂיהָ וְתִפְאֶרֶת לוֹ מִן הָאָדָם, וֶהֱוֵי זָהִיר בְּמִצְוָה קַלָּה כְּבַחֲמוּרָה, שֶׁאֵין אַתָּה יוֹדֵעַ מַתַּן שְׂכָרָן שֶׁל מִצְוֹת, וֶהֱוֵי מְחַשֵּׁב הֶפְסֵד מִצְוָה כְּנֶגֶד שְׂכָרָהּ, וּשְׂכַר עֲבֵרָה כְּנֶגֶד הֶפְסֵדָהּ. הִסְתַּכֵּל בִּשְׁלֹשָׁה דְבָרִים, וְאֵין אַתָּה בָא לִידֵי עֲבֵרָה, דַּע מַה לְמַעְלָה מִמְּךָ, עַיִן רוֹאָה וְאֹזֶן שׁוֹמַעַת, וְכָל מַעֲשֶׂיךָ בְּסֵפֶר נִכְתָּבִים.

ב. רַבָּן גַּמְלִיאֵל בְּנוֹ שֶׁל רַבִּי יְהוּדָה הַנָּשִׂיא אוֹמֵר: יָפֶה תַלְמוּד תּוֹרָה עִם דֶּרֶךְ אֶרֶץ, שֶׁיְּגִיעַת שְׁנֵיהֶם מַשְׁכַּחַת עָוֹן, וְכָל תּוֹרָה

You do not know the gift of reward. The reward for the finite aspect of the mitzvah—its specific effect on the human being—is likewise finite and therefore knowable. The reward for its infinite aspect—the fact that it is the Divine will—is likewise infinite and therefore unknowable.

Even while focusing on and internalizing the particular elements of the *mitzvot*—by which they are "minor" and finite—retain an awareness of their infinite and transcendent element—the fact that they are all equally G-d's infinite will (*Biurim*).

Reflect upon three things. R. Yehudah's reflections do not denigrate man (cf. below 3:1), they beautify him by emphasizing the importance of his deeds (*Magen Avot*).

2. Torah…with *derech eretz* (work). The act of earning a living actualizes the goal of creation, which is to make the *material* world a Divine home. This can only be achieved by those who deal directly with the material world in a sanctified manner.

It is therefore the destiny of most people not to be immersed entirely in the "tent of Torah," since it is only through sanctified interaction with the material world that the purpose of creation is realized (see *Likkutei Sichot*, 30:138).

Derech eretz can also mean etiquette. If a conflict arises between the study or observance of Torah and etiquette, do not be a zealot and ignore protocol, nor should you ignore Torah and zealously embrace protocol. Find a way to harmonize the two without compromising on either (*Chasdei Avot* (BIC)).

CHAPTER TWO

All of Israel have a share in the World to Come, as it says, *Your people are all righteous; they will inherit the Land forever; they are the branch of My planting, the work of My hands in which I take pride.*[1] (*Sanhedrin* 11:1)

---

1. Rabbi [Yehudah the Prince] said: Which is the proper path that man should choose for himself? Whatever brings beauty to he that does it and is beautiful to mankind. Be as careful with a minor mitzvah as with a major one, for you do not know the gift of reward for mitzvot. Consider the loss caused by a mitzvah against its reward, and the gain of a sin against the loss it incurs. Reflect upon three things and you will not come to the hands of sin. Know what is above you: an Eye that sees, an Ear that hears; and that all your deeds are recorded in a Book.

2. Rabban Gamliel, son of R. Yehudah the Prince said: Torah study goes well with *derech eretz* (work), since the toil of both of them

---

1. Beauty. Beauty is created by a harmonious blend of diverse elements. R. Yehudah emphasizes the need for a Divine worship that is multi-dimensional, where man maintains a balance of doing what is beautiful and beneficial for *his* spiritual growth and at the same time focusing on imparting that beauty to others—self-fulfillment coupled with commitment to community (*Biurim*).

Beautiful to mankind. Serve G-d not only with forced obedience but because you appreciate the meaning and beauty of the *mitzvot* (*Chasdei Avot* (*BIC*)). Become a person who *chooses for himself* to serve G-d. The Mishnah can now be read as, *Which is the proper path? That man choose for himself.*

When your self is transformed, when you internalize and understand the Torah, you become beautified and illuminated by it. Your enthusiasm and joy demonstrates the beauty of Torah to those around you (*Biurim*).

Be as careful with a minor mitzvah. When a person serves G-d only out of obedience, he senses no difference between one mitzvah and another. He is focused on the equalizing aspect of the *mitzvot*: the fact that they are all equally the Divine will.

But when he focuses on understanding the *mitzvot* and the effect they have on the human being, he notices the differences between them —some are minor, others major. R. Yehudah therefore warns that even with this recognition be sure to treat a minor mitzvah as seriously as a major one (*Biurim*).

---

1. Isaiah 60:21.

17

שֶׁאֵין עִמָּהּ מְלָאכָה סוֹפָהּ בְּטֵלָה וְגוֹרֶרֶת עָוֹן, וְכָל הָעוֹסְקִים עִם
הַצִּבּוּר יִהְיוּ עוֹסְקִים עִמָּהֶם לְשֵׁם שָׁמַיִם, שֶׁזְּכוּת אֲבוֹתָם
מְסַיַּעְתָּם, וְצִדְקָתָם עוֹמֶדֶת לָעַד, וְאַתֶּם, מַעֲלֶה אֲנִי עֲלֵיכֶם שָׂכָר
הַרְבֵּה כְּאִלּוּ עֲשִׂיתֶם.

ג. הֱווּ זְהִירִין בָּרָשׁוּת, שֶׁאֵין מְקָרְבִין לוֹ לְאָדָם אֶלָּא לְצֹרֶךְ עַצְמָן,
נִרְאִין כְּאוֹהֲבִין בִּשְׁעַת הֲנָאָתָן, וְאֵין עוֹמְדִין לוֹ לְאָדָם בִּשְׁעַת
דָּחֳקוֹ.

ד. הוּא הָיָה אוֹמֵר: עֲשֵׂה רְצוֹנוֹ כִּרְצוֹנְךָ, כְּדֵי שֶׁיַּעֲשֶׂה רְצוֹנְךָ
כִּרְצוֹנוֹ, בַּטֵּל רְצוֹנְךָ מִפְּנֵי רְצוֹנוֹ כְּדֵי שֶׁיְּבַטֵּל רְצוֹן אֲחֵרִים מִפְּנֵי
רְצוֹנֶךָ.

הִלֵּל אוֹמֵר: אַל תִּפְרוֹשׁ מִן הַצִּבּוּר, וְאַל תַּאֲמִין בְּעַצְמָךְ עַד יוֹם
מוֹתָךְ, וְאַל תָּדִין אֶת חֲבֵרָךְ עַד שֶׁתַּגִּיעַ לִמְקוֹמוֹ, וְאַל תֹּאמַר דָּבָר

- **Shmayah:** Love work. RG: But work is good only when it comes along with Torah study.
- **Shmayah:** Abhor leadership. RG: But serve the community anyway for the sake of Heaven.
- **Shmayah:** Do not fraternize with government. RG: Unless it is necessary for you as a leader; and then—be wary (*Midrash Shmuel*).

4. Make your will like His will. Transform your will so that it becomes synonymous with that of G-d's. G-d will then *make your will His will*—your holy desires, such as a yearning for personal and cosmic redemption, will become His manifest and actual will (*Biurim*). Alternatively, strive to transform your will and G-d will assist you in that goal—He will make your will like His will (see *Sfat Emet*).

The will of others. According to *Bar-*

tenura, *others* is a euphemism for G-d—i.e., G-d will set aside His will for yours. G-d will nullify His external will and allow His inner will to be manifest (*Biurim*).

Hillel said. This is Hillel the Elder, cited above (1:12). After citing the sayings of Hillel's descendants who were leaders of the Sanhedrin all the way through Rabban Gamliel III (the last of his descendants in the Mishnaic period), the Mishnah reintroduces Hillel before it continues with his student Rabban Yochanan ben Zakai, below, Mishnah 8 (*Sforno*, intro.).

Not readily heard. Speak clearly so that your words are not misinterpreted (*Mefarshim*). Alternatively, do not say that a certain Torah thought cannot be understood, for in the end, with effort, it can be understood (*R. Moshe Almoshnino*).

banishes misdeed. Any Torah study that is not accompanied by work will ultimately cease and lead to misdeed. All who serve the community should do so for the sake of Heaven. For the merit of their forefathers assists them and their righteousness endures forever. [And G-d says:] I will bestow great reward upon you as if you had accomplished it [alone].

3. Be wary of those in power, for they befriend a person only for their own benefit; they seem to be friends when it is to their advantage, but they do not stand by a man in his hour of need.

4. He used to say: Make your will like His will so that He may make your will as His will; nullify your will before His will, so that He may nullify the will of others before your will.

Hillel said: Do not separate yourself from the community; do not be sure of yourself until the day you die; do not judge your fellowman until you have stood in his place; do not speak that which is not readily heard, but which will ultimately be heard;

Torah...not accompanied by work. The Baal Shem Tov explained this phrase to mean that any Torah study that does not translate into the "work" of loving your fellow will be lost (*Keter Shem Tov*). As the Talmud says of material wealth (*Temurah* 16a): share it or lose it (*Biurim, hosafot; Chasdei Avot*).

For the sake of heaven. I.e., not to don a crown and to say, "Look what I have done for the community" (*Bartenura*).

Merit of their Forefathers. Your success should not make you arrogant, since it is not due to your talent but to the merit of the community's forefathers (*Bartenura*).

As if you had accomplished. Even though the success is due to the merit of the forefathers, I, G-d, will reward you as if you had brought this salvation

to Israel on your own, since your intentions are for the sake of Heaven (*Bartenura*). I will also reward you for those *mitzvot* you failed to fulfill because of your preoccupation with communal duties. I will consider it as if you had done those *mitzvot* (*Rambam*).

3. Be wary of those in power. This can also refer to the powers that control the human being: the mind, the heart, and the animal soul. Be careful with these powers. They may crave things that are to your detriment and yet appear to be your friends. They will manipulate you into thinking that their desire is to your benefit —even your *spiritual* benefit—when, in fact, their advice will ultimately harm you (*Midrash Shmuel* citing *Moharit; Biurim*).

Rabban Gamliel's statements qualify the statements of Shmayah (above 1:10):

שֶׁאִי אֶפְשָׁר לִשְׁמוֹעַ שֶׁסּוֹפוֹ לְהִשָּׁמַע, וְאַל תֹּאמַר לִכְשֶׁאֶפָּנֶה אֶשְׁנֶה, שֶׁמָּא לֹא תִפָּנֶה.

ה. הוּא הָיָה אוֹמֵר: אֵין בּוּר יְרֵא חֵטְא, וְלֹא עַם הָאָרֶץ חָסִיד, וְלֹא הַבַּיְשָׁן לָמֵד, וְלֹא הַקַּפְּדָן מְלַמֵּד, וְלֹא כָל הַמַּרְבֶּה בִסְחוֹרָה מַחְכִּים, וּבְמָקוֹם שֶׁאֵין אֲנָשִׁים, הִשְׁתַּדֵּל לִהְיוֹת אִישׁ.

ו. אַף הוּא רָאָה גֻלְגֹּלֶת אַחַת שֶׁצָּפָה עַל פְּנֵי הַמָּיִם, אָמַר לָהּ: עַל דַּאֲטֵפְתְּ אַטְפוּךְ, וְסוֹף מְטִיפָיִךְ יְטוּפוּן.

ז. הוּא הָיָה אוֹמֵר: מַרְבֶּה בָשָׂר מַרְבֶּה רִמָּה, מַרְבֶּה נְכָסִים מַרְבֶּה דְאָגָה, מַרְבֶּה נָשִׁים מַרְבֶּה כְשָׁפִים, מַרְבֶּה שְׁפָחוֹת מַרְבֶּה זִמָּה,

---

used Pharaoh to derive a lesson, thereby bringing merit to Pharaoh and enabling his tortured soul to be at rest (*Biurim*).

Those who drowned you. According to Arizal, Hillel addressed these words to the Jewish people, saying:

"Not only was Pharaoh drowned —in the end, all the nations that will drown you and persecute you throughout the generations will also be repaid, as was Pharaoh" (*Shaar Maamarei Razal*).

Hillel's words serve as a balm to the broken soul: If Pharaoh, the "great serpent" who struck fear even into the heart of Moshe (*Zohar* 2:34a), met such a humiliating end, certainly all forces of darkness and challenges will meet a similar end. One can therefore let go of despair and sadness and serve G-d with joy (*Biurim*).

7. One's focus in life should be Torah, *mitzvot* and perfection of character. All else should be dealt with

only as necessary—not more. Excess in material things brings harm, while excess in Torah and good deeds brings blessing (*Meiri, Bartenura*).

Increasing flesh. One who eats more than necessary gains body fat that will ultimately be eaten by worms in the grave. This causes great pain to the soul, which must witness the body's decay. As the Talmud says (*Berachot* 18b): "Worms are as painful for the [soul of the] dead as a needle in the flesh of the living" (*Bartenura; Tosfot Yom Tov*).

Even during one's lifetime, overeating increases "worms" in the sense of increased susceptibility to illness (*Binah L'itim*).

Increasing wives. [Although polygamy was legally permitted in Mishnaic times, the Mishnah discourages it.] Polygamy causes each wife to vie for the husband's love. Each wife will resort to drastic measures—even sorcery—to cause the husband to hate the other wife. The husband should

and do not say, "When I am free, I will study," for perhaps you will never be free.

5. He used to say: An empty person cannot be sin-fearing, nor can an ignoramus be pious; the bashful person cannot learn, nor can the short-tempered teach; neither can all who are excessively occupied in trade become wise; and in a place where there are no men, strive to be a man.

6. He also saw a skull floating on the water. He said to it: "Because you drowned others, you were drowned; and ultimately those who drowned you will drown."

7. He used to say: Increasing flesh, increases worms; increasing possessions, increases worry; increasing wives, increases sorcery; in-

---

5. An empty person cannot be sin-fearing. A person who is empty of Torah—even if he studies it all the time (*Mili d'Chasiduta*)—may attain fear of *punishment*, but he lacks the spiritual sensitivity to become fearful of and repelled by sin itself (*Tiferet Yisrael*; see *Maharal*).

Nor can an ignoramus be pious. An ignoramus cannot be pious in his actions, since, even if well-intentioned and repelled by sin, he is ignorant of the laws (*Divrei Shaul*).

Where there are no men, strive to be a man. Like Pinchas, stand up for the right thing even if no one else does (see *HaChasid*). Additionally, do not feel that since there is no one greater than you in your immediate surrounding—or even in the rest of the world (*R. Yonah*)—you need not improve yourself. Even *where there are no men, strive to be a man* and acquire perfection (*Midrash Shmuel*).

6. Because you drowned others you

were drowned. Hillel makes the point that a person is punished in a manner that mirrors the sin he committed (see *Sotah* 8b). The inventor of new villainous tactics will himself be harmed by them. Conversely, the inventor of a positive thing will ultimately benefit from it himself (*Rambam*).

A skull. Rambam's grandson cites "the early ones" as saying that this skull was the head of Pharaoh, who ordered the drowning of all Jewish male newborns (see Exodus 1:22).

Hillel's soul contained a spark of Moshe. (He was therefore humble like Moshe and lived 120 years like Moshe.) Like Moshe, Hillel confronts Pharaoh (*Midrash David, Arizal*).

He said to it. Why would Hillel rebuke a dead person who was no longer able to rectify his deeds? When Hillel saw that Heaven had caused Pharaoh's skull to cross his path, he realized that it was time for Pharaoh to finally find peace. He therefore

מַרְבֶּה עֲבָדִים מַרְבֶּה גָזֵל. מַרְבֶּה תוֹרָה מַרְבֶּה חַיִּים, מַרְבֶּה יְשִׁיבָה מַרְבֶּה חָכְמָה, מַרְבֶּה עֵצָה מַרְבֶּה תְבוּנָה, מַרְבֶּה צְדָקָה מַרְבֶּה שָׁלוֹם. קָנָה שֵׁם טוֹב קָנָה לְעַצְמוֹ, קָנָה לוֹ דִּבְרֵי תוֹרָה קָנָה לוֹ חַיֵּי הָעוֹלָם הַבָּא.

ח. רַבָּן יוֹחָנָן בֶּן זַכַּאי קִבֵּל מֵהִלֵּל וּמִשַּׁמַּאי. הוּא הָיָה אוֹמֵר: אִם לָמַדְתָּ תוֹרָה הַרְבֵּה, אַל תַּחֲזִיק טוֹבָה לְעַצְמָךְ, כִּי לְכָךְ נוֹצָרְתָּ.

ט. חֲמִשָּׁה תַלְמִידִים הָיוּ לוֹ לְרַבָּן יוֹחָנָן בֶּן זַכַּאי, וְאֵלּוּ הֵן: רַבִּי אֱלִיעֶזֶר בֶּן הוֹרְקְנוֹס, וְרַבִּי יְהוֹשֻׁעַ בֶּן חֲנַנְיָא, וְרַבִּי יוֹסֵי הַכֹּהֵן, וְרַבִּי שִׁמְעוֹן בֶּן נְתַנְאֵל, וְרַבִּי אֶלְעָזָר בֶּן עֲרָךְ. הוּא הָיָה מוֹנֶה שְׁבָחָם. רַבִּי אֱלִיעֶזֶר בֶּן הוֹרְקְנוֹס בּוֹר סוּד שֶׁאֵינוֹ מְאַבֵּד טִפָּה, רַבִּי יְהוֹשֻׁעַ בֶּן חֲנַנְיָא אַשְׁרֵי יוֹלַדְתּוֹ, רַבִּי יוֹסֵי הַכֹּהֵן חָסִיד,

---

out the books of the Mishnah (*Meiri*).

Praiseworthy. Every person has a unique quality in which he can "outweigh" all others. Like the five students of R. Yochanan, each person should strive to cultivate this quality and bring it to light (*Biurim*; see *Maharal* and *Maharam Shik*).

Does not lose a drop. Similarly, R. Eliezer does not forget anything he learns (*Bartenura*).

Fortunate is she who bore him. R. Yehoshua developed extraordinarily fine character and was beloved and respected by all. This prompted all to say: "Fortunate is she that bore him" (*Rambam*). In addition, it was because of his mother that he achieved such greatness. While carrying him in her

womb, she went to every study hall in her city and asked the Sages to pray that he become a sage. She also kept the infant in the study hall so that only holy words would enter his ears (*Bartenura*; see J.T., *Yevamot* 1:6).

● At the moment a person is born, his entire life is before him. He has the potential to live a completely meaningful life. Whether he will *actualize* this potential is up to him. R. Yehoshua actualized the potential for perfection that he possessed at birth. R. Yochanan alludes to this quality by referring to his birth (*Biurim*).

Chasid. A *chasid* is one who goes beyond the letter of the law (*Bartenura*) and who is willing to harm himself for the benefit of another (see *Tosfot Niddah* 17a s.v. *sorfan chasid*; see introduction).

creasing maidservants, increases lewdness; increasing servants, increases thievery. Increasing Torah [study], increases life; increasing study [with colleagues], increases wisdom; increasing counsel, increases understanding; increasing charity, increases peace. One who has acquired a good name, has acquired it for himself; one who has acquired for himself Torah knowledge has acquired for himself life in the World to Come.

8. Rabban Yochanan ben Zakkai received from Hillel and Shammai. He used to say: If you have learned much Torah, do not take credit for yourself, since it is for this that you were formed.

9. Rabban Yochanan ben Zakkai had five [outstanding] disciples, and they were: R. Eliezer ben Horkenus, R. Yehoshua ben Chananya, R. Yosay the Kohen, R. Shimon ben Netanel, and R. Elazar ben Arach. He used to enumerate their praiseworthy qualities: R. Eliezer ben Horkenus: a cemented cistern that does not lose a drop; R. Yehoshua ben Chananya: fortunate is she who bore him; R. Yosay the Kohen: a *chasid*; R. Shimon ben

---

therefore think twice before creating such a condition for which he is ultimately responsible (see *R. Yonah*).

Study [with colleagues]. Translation follows Maharal. Alternatively, study with *students* increases wisdom, since they sharpen the teacher's mind *(Bartenura)*.

Counsel...understanding. One who takes counsel from others gains understanding *(Mefarshim)*. Also, one who considers how to best counsel *others* will gain understanding that can be applied to his own life *(student of Ritva)*.

For himself. All worldly acquisitions do not remain with a person after death and must be passed on to others. A good name, however, outlives

the person. Yet even a good name does not last forever. Only one who acquires Torah acquires something eternal *(R. Moshe Alashkar)*.

8. Do not take credit. A characteristic can only be a source of pride if its absence is not considered a deficiency. One can take pride in an extraordinary talent, since its absence is not considered a defect. But one cannot take pride in having two arms. Similarly, knowledge of Torah should not be a source of pride, since its absence would render the person deficient *(Knesset Yisrael)*.

9. Five disciples. Of his many disciples, these five achieved extraordinary success and received the oral tradition from him. They are the first and primary sages cited through-

רַבִּי שִׁמְעוֹן בֶּן נְתַנְאֵל יְרֵא חֵטְא, וְרַבִּי אֶלְעָזָר בֶּן עֲרָךְ כְּמַעְיָן הַמִּתְגַּבֵּר.

הוּא הָיָה אוֹמֵר: אִם יִהְיוּ כָּל חַכְמֵי יִשְׂרָאֵל בְּכַף מֹאזְנַיִם, וֶאֱלִיעֶזֶר בֶּן הוֹרְקְנוֹס בְּכַף שְׁנִיָּה, מַכְרִיעַ אֶת כֻּלָּם. אַבָּא שָׁאוּל אוֹמֵר מִשְּׁמוֹ: אִם יִהְיוּ כָּל חַכְמֵי יִשְׂרָאֵל בְּכַף מֹאזְנַיִם וֶאֱלִיעֶזֶר בֶּן הוֹרְקְנוֹס אַף עִמָּהֶם, וְאֶלְעָזָר בֶּן עֲרָךְ בְּכַף שְׁנִיָּה, מַכְרִיעַ אֶת כֻּלָּם.

י. אָמַר לָהֶם: צְאוּ וּרְאוּ אֵיזוֹ הִיא דֶרֶךְ טוֹבָה שֶׁיִּדְבַּק בָּהּ הָאָדָם. רַבִּי אֱלִיעֶזֶר אוֹמֵר: עַיִן טוֹבָה. רַבִּי יְהוֹשֻׁעַ אוֹמֵר: חָבֵר טוֹב. רַבִּי יוֹסֵי אוֹמֵר: שָׁכֵן טוֹב. רַבִּי שִׁמְעוֹן אוֹמֵר: הָרוֹאֶה אֶת הַנּוֹלָד. רַבִּי אֶלְעָזָר אוֹמֵר: לֵב טוֹב. אָמַר לָהֶם: רוֹאֶה אֲנִי אֶת דִּבְרֵי אֶלְעָזָר בֶּן עֲרָךְ מִדִּבְרֵיכֶם, שֶׁבִּכְלַל דְּבָרָיו דִּבְרֵיכֶם.

אָמַר לָהֶם: צְאוּ וּרְאוּ אֵיזוֹ הִיא דֶרֶךְ רָעָה שֶׁיִּתְרַחֵק מִמֶּנָּה הָאָדָם.

רַבִּי אֱלִיעֶזֶר אוֹמֵר: עַיִן רָעָה. רַבִּי יְהוֹשֻׁעַ אוֹמֵר: חָבֵר רָע. רַבִּי יוֹסֵי אוֹמֵר: שָׁכֵן רָע. רַבִּי שִׁמְעוֹן אוֹמֵר: הַלֹּוֶה וְאֵינוֹ מְשַׁלֵּם, אֶחָד הַלֹּוֶה מִן הָאָדָם כְּלֹוֶה מִן הַמָּקוֹם, שֶׁנֶּאֱמַר: לֹוֶה רָשָׁע וְלֹא יְשַׁלֵּם, וְצַדִּיק חוֹנֵן וְנוֹתֵן. רַבִּי אֶלְעָזָר אוֹמֵר: לֵב רָע. אָמַר לָהֶם: רוֹאֶה אֲנִי אֶת דִּבְרֵי אֶלְעָזָר בֶּן עֲרָךְ מִדִּבְרֵיכֶם, שֶׁבִּכְלַל דְּבָרָיו דִּבְרֵיכֶם.

הֵם אָמְרוּ שְׁלֹשָׁה דְבָרִים. רַבִּי אֱלִיעֶזֶר אוֹמֵר: יְהִי כְבוֹד חֲבֵרְךָ

---

loves all (*Meiri*).

His words include your own. The heart is the root of all deeds and thoughts. From a good heart will emerge good traits (*Bartenura*).

Bad eye. He scorns all that he has and yearns for what he has not (*Rambam*).

One who borrows from G-d. When a loan is not repaid, G-d compensates the lender. "The wicked one borrows and does not repay; but the Right-

eous One"—i.e., G-d—"acts graciously and gives" the lender what he has lost (*Rambam*).

As dear...as your own. It is not enough to merely *act* respectfully toward your fellow—his honor must be as dear to you as your own. You must feel his shame (*Biurim*). If he is being shamed, stand up for his honor as you would for your own (*Midrash Shmuel*).

Honor; do not be easily angered. If

Netanel: sin-fearing; and R. Elazar ben Arach: like a fountain flowing with ever-increasing strength.

He used to say: If all the Sages of Israel were on one side of the scale, and Eliezer ben Horkenus on the other, he would outweigh them all. Abba Shaul said in his name: If all the Sages of Israel, including Eliezer ben Horkenus, were on one side of the scale, and Elazar ben Arach on the other, he would outweigh them all.

10. He said to them: Go out and see which is the good path to which man should cleave. R. Eliezer said: A good eye. R. Yehoshua said: A good friend. R. Yosay said: A good neighbor. R. Shimon said: One who foresees the consequences [of his actions]. R. Elazar said: A good heart. [Rabban Yochanan ben Zakkai] said to them: I prefer the words of Elazar ben Arach to all of yours, for his words include your own.

He said to them: Go out and see which is the evil path from which a man should keep away.

R. Eliezer said: A bad eye. R. Yehoshua said: A bad friend. R. Yosay said: A bad neighbor. R. Shimon said: He who borrows and does not repay. One who borrows from man is as one who borrows from G-d, as it says: *The wicked one borrows and does not repay, but the Righteous One acts graciously and gives.*[2] R. Elazar said: An evil heart. [Rabban Yochanan ben Zakkai] said to them: I prefer the words of Elazar ben Arach to all of yours, for his words include your own.

They [each] said three things. R. Eliezer said: Let the honor of your fellow be as dear to you as your own; do not be easily an-

---

A fountain. He expanded upon what he learned from his teachers (*Mefarshim*).

Abba Shaul. In memory and knowledge, Eliezer ben Horkenus outweighed them all; but in analytical prowess and acuity, Elazar ben Arach was superior (*R. Yonah*).

10. Cleave. Instead of cleaving moderately to *all* good attributes, cleave fully to one specific attribute. You will then more easily acquire the others (*R. Yonah*).

Good eye. A person with a good eye enjoys seeing the good fortune of others. He is therefore beloved to all and

---

2. Psalms 37:21.

חָבִיב עָלֶיךָ כְּשֶׁלָּךְ, וְאַל תְּהִי נוֹחַ לִכְעוֹס. וְשׁוּב יוֹם אֶחָד לִפְנֵי מִיתָתָךְ. וֶהֱוֵי מִתְחַמֵּם כְּנֶגֶד אוּרָן שֶׁל חֲכָמִים, וֶהֱוֵי זָהִיר בְּגַחַלְתָּן שֶׁלֹּא תִכָּוֶה, שֶׁנְּשִׁיכָתָן נְשִׁיכַת שׁוּעָל, וַעֲקִיצָתָן עֲקִיצַת עַקְרָב, וּלְחִישָׁתָן לְחִישַׁת שָׂרָף, וְכָל דִּבְרֵיהֶם כְּגַחֲלֵי אֵשׁ.

יא. רַבִּי יְהוֹשֻׁעַ אוֹמֵר: עַיִן הָרָע, וְיֵצֶר הָרָע, וְשִׂנְאַת הַבְּרִיּוֹת, מוֹצִיאִין אֶת הָאָדָם מִן הָעוֹלָם.

יב. רַבִּי יוֹסֵי אוֹמֵר: יְהִי מָמוֹן חֲבֵרְךָ חָבִיב עָלֶיךָ כְּשֶׁלָּךְ. וְהַתְקֵן עַצְמְךָ לִלְמֹד תּוֹרָה, שֶׁאֵינָהּ יְרֻשָּׁה לָךְ. וְכָל מַעֲשֶׂיךָ יִהְיוּ לְשֵׁם שָׁמָיִם.

יג. רַבִּי שִׁמְעוֹן אוֹמֵר: הֱוֵי זָהִיר בִּקְרִיאַת שְׁמַע וּבִתְפִלָּה. וּכְשֶׁאַתָּה מִתְפַּלֵּל, אַל תַּעַשׂ תְּפִלָּתְךָ קֶבַע, אֶלָּא רַחֲמִים וְתַחֲנוּנִים לִפְנֵי הַמָּקוֹם, שֶׁנֶּאֱמַר: כִּי חַנּוּן וְרַחוּם הוּא, אֶרֶךְ

---

12. Money of your fellowman. It is not enough to *treat* the money of your fellow as you would your own, you must *feel* as concerned about his money as you are about your own (*Biurim*). Just as you would not want a negative rumor to circulate regarding your property, do not allow the same to occur to your fellow's (*Avot d'Rabbi Nattan*).

Not an inheritance. Even a descendant of Torah sages should not assume that the Torah will automatically become his: "Many rivers have gone dry; many rocks have given water" (*Meiri*).

● In truth the Torah is an inheritance [in the sense that every Jew has the right and ability to study Torah and receives some aspects from Torah without any effort]. But to *acquire* the Torah—to internalize it and un-

derstand it—one must fix and condition oneself. This fixing is achieved by attaining the forty-eight qualities though which the Torah is acquired, enumerated below 6:6 (*Biurim*; see *R. Yonah*).

For the sake of Heaven. Engage in business to earn money with which to support your family and to give charity; eat and sleep in order to have strength to do *mitzvot*, etc. (see *Mefarshim*).

13. Be meticulous. Be sure to recite each prayer within its designated time (e.g., the morning *Shema* within the first three hours of the day) (*Rashi*).

He is gracious. Do not say, "Why would G-d listen to the prayers of a sinner like me?" G-d is gracious and compassionate and listens to all who pray to Him (*Knesset Yisrael*).

gered; and repent one day before your death. Warm yourself by the fire of the sages, but beware of their glowing embers lest you be burnt, for their bite is the bite of a fox, their sting is the sting of a scorpion, their hiss is the hiss of a serpent, and all their words are like fiery coals.

11. R. Yehoshua said: An evil eye, an evil inclination, and hatred of others drive a man from the world.

12. R. Yosay said: Let the money of your fellowman be as dear to you as your own; fix yourself for the study of Torah, for it does not come to you through inheritance; and let all your deeds be for the sake of Heaven.

13. R. Shimon said: Be meticulous in reading the *Shema* and in prayer. When you pray, do not make your prayer a routine [perfunctory] act, but an entreaty for mercy and supplication before the Omnipresent, as it says: *For He is gracious and compassionate, slow to anger and abounding in lovingkindness, and re-*

---

you are angered easily you will inevitably dishonor your fellow (*Rashi*). And if you cherish the honor of your fellow, you will be slow to anger (*Midrash Shmuel*). R. Eliezer's first two dictums can therefore be considered as one (*Rashi*).

Repent one day before your death. Return to your true, Divine-oriented self each day as if it were your last (see *Avot d'Rabbi Nattan*).

THE TEACHER-STUDENT DYNAMIC. A teacher is like a fire: warm yourself by his wisdom but do not get too close. Maintain the proper distance and refrain from acting too familiarly with the teacher, even when the teacher behaves familiarly with him. Otherwise, he "burns up" and destroys the relationship (*Rambam*).

Fox. The various animals and injuries

they cause symbolize different levels of damage caused by the master's displeasure (see *Maharal*; *Midrash Shmuel*).

11. Evil eye. Jealousy (*R. Yonah*).

Evil inclination. Hedonism (*Rambam*).

Hatred of others. I.e., senseless hatred, (*Rashi*), one that is caused not by any offense committed by the hated party but by the egoism of the hater, who cannot stand the sight of another (see *On Ahavat Yisrael—Heichaltzu 5659*).

Drive a man from the world. One who possesses these traits will be driven from the world (*Rambam*) and will drive *others* from the world (*Magen Avot*).

אַפַּיִם וְרַב חֶסֶד, וְנִחָם עַל הָרָעָה. וְאַל תְּהִי רָשָׁע בִּפְנֵי עַצְמֶךָ.

יד. רַבִּי אֶלְעָזָר אוֹמֵר: הֱוֵי שָׁקוּד לִלְמוֹד תּוֹרָה. וְדַע מַה שֶׁתָּשִׁיב לְאֶפִּיקוֹרוֹס. וְדַע לִפְנֵי מִי אַתָּה עָמֵל, וּמִי הוּא בַּעַל מְלַאכְתֶּךָ שֶׁיְּשַׁלֵּם לָךְ שְׂכַר פְּעֻלָּתֶךָ.

טו. רַבִּי טַרְפוֹן אוֹמֵר: הַיּוֹם קָצֵר, וְהַמְּלָאכָה מְרֻבָּה, וְהַפּוֹעֲלִים עֲצֵלִים, וְהַשָּׂכָר הַרְבֵּה, וּבַעַל הַבַּיִת דּוֹחֵק.

טז. הוּא הָיָה אוֹמֵר: לֹא עָלֶיךָ הַמְּלָאכָה לִגְמוֹר, וְלֹא אַתָּה בֶּן חוֹרִין לְהִבָּטֵל מִמֶּנָּה, אִם לָמַדְתָּ תּוֹרָה הַרְבֵּה, נוֹתְנִין לָךְ שָׂכָר הַרְבֵּה, וְנֶאֱמָן הוּא בַּעַל מְלַאכְתֶּךָ שֶׁיְּשַׁלֵּם לָךְ שְׂכַר פְּעֻלָּתֶךָ, וְדַע שֶׁמַּתַּן שְׂכָרָן שֶׁל צַדִּיקִים לֶעָתִיד לָבֹא.

רַבִּי חֲנַנְיָא בֶּן עֲקַשְׁיָא אוֹמֵר: רָצָה הַקָּדוֹשׁ בָּרוּךְ הוּא לְזַכּוֹת אֶת יִשְׂרָאֵל, לְפִיכָךְ הִרְבָּה לָהֶם תּוֹרָה וּמִצְוֹת, שֶׁנֶּאֱמַר: יְיָ חָפֵץ לְמַעַן צִדְקוֹ, יַגְדִּיל תּוֹרָה וְיַאְדִּיר.

---

15. The day is short. The human lifespan is compared to a shadow. Not a permanent shadow, like that of a tree or a wall, but fleeting, like that of a bird flying through the sky (Rashi on Psalms 144:4).

The work is much. The Torah's measure is "longer than the earth and wider than the sea" (Job 11:9).

● R. Tarfon addresses the person who does not force himself to go beyond his natural inclination. To stretch one's limits is *much work*, and *the workmen are lazy* in this regard—but *the reward is great*, far more than what is received for serving G-d within one's natural limits. *And the Master is*

pressing—G-d makes it hard; not, G-d forbid, to torment the workmen, but to allow them the gift of self-actualization (*Biurim*).

16. It is not your obligation to complete the work. This Mishnah is a sequel to the previous one: If the Torah is so vast and I will not complete it in any case, nor will I will ever reach perfection—why not give up altogether?

To this R. Tarfon says: You are not obligated to complete the task, but neither are you free to desist from it (*Midrash Shmuel*). The previous Mishnah challenges and demands; this Mishnah encourages and comforts (*Magen Avot*).

nounces evil [decrees].[3] And do not view yourself as a wicked person.

14. R. Elazar said: Be diligent in the study of Torah; know what to respond to a heretic; and know before Whom you toil, and Who your Employer is that will pay you the reward of your labor.

15. R. Tarfon said: The day is short, the work is much, the workmen are lazy, the reward is great, and the Master is pressing.

16. He used to say: It is not your obligation to complete the work, but neither are you free to desist from it; if you have studied much Torah, they will give you much reward; and your Employer is trustworthy to pay you the reward for your labor, but know that the giving of reward to the righteous will be in the World to Come.

Rabbi Chananyah ben Akashya said: The Holy One, blessed be He, wished to make Israel meritorious. He therefore increased for them Torah and mitzvot, as it says: *G-d desired, for the sake of his [Israel's] righteousness, to make the Torah great and glorious.*[4] (*Makkot* 3:16)

Do not view yourself as a wicked person. Self-deprecating thoughts are only appropriate if they lead to remorse and reform. But if they impede fulfillment of *mitzvot*—"A sinner like me should do a mitzvah?"—their source cannot be holy (see *Tanya* chs. 27-31 and *Knesset Yisrael*).

14. Diligent study. R. Elazar's unique quality was in building upon the ideas of his teachers. For him it was therefore especially important to diligently study and review the teachings of his masters so that he would not lose sight of their words in his effort to expand upon them (*Biurim*).

Know what to respond. Study the depth and profundity of Torah diligently, in a way that will provide you with the answers to the questions of cynics—including the voice of cynicism within yourself. One must not allow falsehood to go unchallenged (*Maharal*).

Reward of your labor. G-d repays you according to the effort you invest, not according to what you accomplish.

Hence, "the reward of *your* labor," even if it accomplishes less than the labor of a more capable fellow (*Midrash Shmuel*).

---

3. Joel 2:13.   4. Isaiah 42:21.

פֶּרֶק שְׁלִישִׁי

כָּל יִשְׂרָאֵל יֵשׁ לָהֶם חֵלֶק לְעוֹלָם הַבָּא, שֶׁנֶּאֱמַר: וְעַמֵּךְ כֻּלָּם צַדִּיקִים, לְעוֹלָם יִירְשׁוּ אָרֶץ, נֵצֶר מַטָּעַי מַעֲשֵׂה יָדַי לְהִתְפָּאֵר.

א. עֲקַבְיָא בֶּן מַהֲלַלְאֵל אוֹמֵר: הִסְתַּכֵּל בִּשְׁלֹשָׁה דְבָרִים, וְאֵין אַתָּה בָא לִידֵי עֲבֵרָה. דַּע מֵאַיִן בָּאתָ, וּלְאָן אַתָּה הוֹלֵךְ, וְלִפְנֵי מִי אַתָּה עָתִיד לִתֵּן דִּין וְחֶשְׁבּוֹן. מֵאַיִן בָּאתָ: מִטִּפָּה סְרוּחָה. וּלְאָן אַתָּה הוֹלֵךְ: לִמְקוֹם עָפָר רִמָּה וְתוֹלֵעָה. וְלִפְנֵי מִי אַתָּה עָתִיד לִתֵּן דִּין וְחֶשְׁבּוֹן: לִפְנֵי מֶלֶךְ מַלְכֵי הַמְּלָכִים הַקָּדוֹשׁ בָּרוּךְ הוּא.

ב. רַבִּי חֲנִינָא סְגַן הַכֹּהֲנִים אוֹמֵר: הֱוֵי מִתְפַּלֵּל בִּשְׁלוֹמָהּ שֶׁל מַלְכוּת, שֶׁאִלְמָלֵא מוֹרָאָהּ, אִישׁ אֶת רֵעֵהוּ חַיִּים בְּלָעוֹ.

רַבִּי חֲנִינָא בֶּן תְּרַדְיוֹן אוֹמֵר: שְׁנַיִם שֶׁיּוֹשְׁבִין וְאֵין בֵּינֵיהֶם דִּבְרֵי תוֹרָה, הֲרֵי זֶה מוֹשַׁב לֵצִים, שֶׁנֶּאֱמַר: וּבְמוֹשַׁב לֵצִים לֹא יָשָׁב. אֲבָל שְׁנַיִם שֶׁיּוֹשְׁבִין וְיֵשׁ בֵּינֵיהֶם דִּבְרֵי תוֹרָה, שְׁכִינָה שְׁרוּיָה בֵינֵיהֶם, שֶׁנֶּאֱמַר: אָז נִדְבְּרוּ יִרְאֵי יְיָ אִישׁ אֶל רֵעֵהוּ,

---

time—is better than anarchy (*Sforno*), where every person is forced to spend his life fending for his very existence (*Meiri*).

Pray also for the "welfare" of the Divine attribute of kingship, which is synonymous with *Shechinah*, the Divine presence (*Ritva*).

● Without a deep sense of awe for the kingdom of Heaven a successful and scholarly person might dismiss those he considers lacking in scholarship or deeds. He sees no value in their existence and can view them only as accessories to his needs. He "swallows them alive," denying them their own identity.

Only the fear of Divine kingship, before Whom small and great are equal, can cure him of his arrogance. Such a person must pray that G-d have mercy on him and help him to perceive the kingship of Heaven (*Biurim*).

No words of Torah...between them. Even if they study Torah but do not exchange words of Torah with *each other*, the Divine presence does not rest upon them, since they lack the humility to recognize that they can gain insight from each other. Each one *scoffs* at the knowledge of the other (*Midrash Shmuel*).

CHAPTER THREE

All of Israel have a share in the World to Come, as it says, *Your people are all righteous; they will inherit the Land forever; they are the branch of My planting, the work of My hands in which I take pride.*[1] (*Sanhedrin* 11:1)

---

1. Akavya ben Mahalalel said: Reflect upon three things and you will not come to the hands of sin: Know from whence you came, where you are going, and before Whom you are destined to give a judgment and an accounting. "From whence you came"—from a putrid drop. "Where you are going"—to a place of dust, maggots and worms. "And before whom you are destined to give a judgment and an accounting"—before the supreme King of kings, the Holy One, blessed be He.

2. R. Chanina, the deputy High-Priest, said: Pray for the welfare of the kingdom, for were it not for the fear of it, a man would swallow his fellow alive.

   R. Chanina ben Tradyon said: When two people sit together and no words of Torah are exchanged between them, they are a company of scoffers, as it says: *He does not sit in the company of scoffers*[2] *[rather, his desire is the Torah of G-d].* But if two people sit together and do exchange words of Torah, the Divine Presence rests between them, as it says: *Then the G-d-fearing conversed, a man with his fellow, and G-d listened and heard, and a*

---

1. Three things. Recognize your humble beginnings and you will be humbled; envision your end and you will despise transient pleasures; ponder the awesomeness of He who commanded the *mitzvot* and you will swiftly fulfill His commands. With these three thoughts in mind you will never act improperly (*Rambam*).

Judgment and accounting. When a person stands before the heavenly court he is asked to judge certain mis-

deeds. Unknown to him is the fact that these are the very misdeeds that he committed. When he pronounces judgment, he pronounces judgment upon himself.

Hence, a person first *gives a judgment* and then *an accounting* is made regarding him (*Midrash Shmuel*; see below, Mishnah 16).

2. Kingdom. Even the rule of a corrupt king—like the majority of Jewish kings during R. Chanina's life-

---

1. Isaiah 60:21. 2. Psalms 1:1.

וַיַּקְשֵׁב יְיָ וַיִּשְׁמָע, וַיִּכָּתֵב סֵפֶר זִכָּרוֹן לְפָנָיו לְיִרְאֵי יְיָ וּלְחשְׁבֵי שְׁמוֹ. אֵין לִי אֶלָּא שְׁנַיִם, מִנַּיִן אֲפִילוּ אֶחָד שֶׁיּוֹשֵׁב וְעוֹסֵק בַּתּוֹרָה שֶׁהַקָּדוֹשׁ בָּרוּךְ הוּא קוֹבֵעַ לוֹ שָׂכָר, שֶׁנֶּאֱמַר: יֵשֵׁב בָּדָד וְיִדֹּם כִּי נָטַל עָלָיו.

ג. רַבִּי שִׁמְעוֹן אוֹמֵר: שְׁלשָׁה שֶׁאָכְלוּ עַל שֻׁלְחָן אֶחָד, וְלֹא אָמְרוּ עָלָיו דִּבְרֵי תוֹרָה, כְּאִלּוּ אָכְלוּ מִזִּבְחֵי מֵתִים, שֶׁנֶּאֱמַר: כִּי כָּל שֻׁלְחָנוֹת מָלְאוּ קִיא צוֹאָה בְּלִי מָקוֹם. אֲבָל שְׁלשָׁה שֶׁאָכְלוּ עַל שֻׁלְחָן אֶחָד וְאָמְרוּ עָלָיו דִּבְרֵי תוֹרָה, כְּאִלּוּ אָכְלוּ מִשֻּׁלְחָנוֹ שֶׁל מָקוֹם, שֶׁנֶּאֱמַר: וַיְדַבֵּר אֵלַי, זֶה הַשֻּׁלְחָן אֲשֶׁר לִפְנֵי יְיָ:

ד. רַבִּי חֲנִינָא בֶּן חֲכִינַאי אוֹמֵר: הַנֵּעוֹר בַּלַּיְלָה, וְהַמְהַלֵּךְ בַּדֶּרֶךְ יְחִידִי, וּמְפַנֶּה לִבּוֹ לְבַטָּלָה, הֲרֵי זֶה מִתְחַיֵּב בְּנַפְשׁוֹ.

ה. רַבִּי נְחוּנְיָא בֶּן הַקָּנָה אוֹמֵר: כָּל הַמְקַבֵּל עָלָיו עוֹל תּוֹרָה, מַעֲבִירִין מִמֶּנּוּ עוֹל מַלְכוּת וְעוֹל דֶּרֶךְ אֶרֶץ, וְכָל הַפּוֹרֵק מִמֶּנּוּ עוֹל תּוֹרָה, נוֹתְנִין עָלָיו עוֹל מַלְכוּת וְעוֹל דֶּרֶךְ אֶרֶץ.

---

alone. One is especially required to study Torah in these circumstances, since one is free of disturbances (*R. Yonah*). Furthermore, these circumstances present spiritual and physical dangers and therefore require Torah study as a protective measure (see *Bartenura*).

● A homiletic interpretation: One who is "awake at night" refers to one who is somehow immune to the darkness that engulfs the world of Exile. But he "travels alone"—he arrogantly thinks that he is the only one on this path. He is content with his own happiness and does not seek to help others to achieve the same spiritual consciousness. In the end, the Mishnah predicts, he will turn his heart to idleness (see *Midrash Shmuel* and *Likkutei Battar Likkutei*).

5. Yoke of Torah. Even if mundane burdens distract you from study, strengthen yourself and study by accepting the "yoke" of Torah.

By transcending mundane worries you will merit their disappearance. But if you decrease your Torah study to better care for your mundane needs, those needs will only increase (*Biurim*; see *Binah L'itim*).

Yoke of mundane cares. Even if you still have to engage in mundane affairs, you will be freed of the *yoke* and worry that usually attends such involvement (*R. Mendel of Kotzk* cited in *Emet Mi-Kotzk Titzmach #299*).

*book of remembrance was written before Him for those who fear
G-d and meditate upon His Name.*[3] From this verse we learn
only that it is so with regard to two people; from where do we
learn that even when one person sits and engages in Torah, the
Holy One, blessed be He, sets a reward for him? From the
verse: *He sits alone in stillness; indeed, he takes [the reward] unto
himself.*[4]

3. R. Shimon said: Three who ate at one table and did not speak
words of Torah upon it, it is as if they had eaten of sacrifices to
the dead [idols], for it is stated: *Indeed, all tables are full of filthy
vomit [when] there is no [mention of] G-d.*[5] But three who ate at
one table and did speak words of Torah upon it, it is as if they
had eaten from the table of G-d, for it is stated: *And he said to
me, this is the table that is before G-d.*[6]

4. R. Chanina ben Chachina'ey said: One who is awake at night or
travels on the path alone, and turns his heart to idleness bears
guilt for [the loss of] his life.

5. R. Nechunya ben Hakanah said: Whoever takes the yoke of Torah upon himself—the yoke of government and the yoke of
mundane cares are removed from him.[7] But whoever casts off the
yoke of Torah from himself—the yoke of government and the
yoke of mundane cares are imposed upon him.

Meditate upon His Name. They attain the level of study in which they
"meditate upon His Name"—they
recognize the Name of G-d in each
word of Torah (*Biurim;* see *Ramban*
intro. to Commentary on Torah).

3. THE TABLE OF G-D. This Mishnah
describes the effect and influence that
the Torah can have on the world.
When a person speaks words of Torah during a meal, the mundane table
is uplifted and it becomes a table of

G-d. What appear to be opposites—a
mundane table and Divinity—are
unified through the power of Torah
(*Biurim*).

Sacrifices of the dead. Without Torah—without granting the meal any
purpose higher than self-gratification
—the table remains "dead," since it
lacks the life and vitality of holiness
(*Biurim*).

4. One who is awake...travels...

---

3. Malachi 2:16.   4. Lamentations 3:28.   5. Isaiah 28:8.   6. Ezekiel 41:22.   7. I.e., the
community bears the burden of his obligation for him.

ו. רַבִּי חֲלַפְתָּא בֶּן דּוֹסָא אִישׁ כְּפַר חֲנַנְיָא אוֹמֵר: עֲשָׂרָה שֶׁיּוֹשְׁבִין
וְעוֹסְקִין בַּתּוֹרָה, שְׁכִינָה שְׁרוּיָה בֵינֵיהֶם, שֶׁנֶּאֱמַר: אֱלֹהִים נִצָּב
בַּעֲדַת אֵל. וּמִנַּיִן אֲפִילוּ חֲמִשָּׁה, שֶׁנֶּאֱמַר: וַאֲגֻדָּתוֹ עַל אֶרֶץ יְסָדָהּ.
וּמִנַּיִן אֲפִילוּ שְׁלֹשָׁה, שֶׁנֶּאֱמַר: בְּקֶרֶב אֱלֹהִים יִשְׁפֹּט. וּמִנַּיִן אֲפִילוּ
שְׁנַיִם, שֶׁנֶּאֱמַר: אָז נִדְבְּרוּ יִרְאֵי יְיָ אִישׁ אֶל רֵעֵהוּ, וַיַּקְשֵׁב יְיָ
וַיִּשְׁמָע. וּמִנַּיִן אֲפִילוּ אֶחָד, שֶׁנֶּאֱמַר: בְּכָל הַמָּקוֹם אֲשֶׁר אַזְכִּיר אֶת
שְׁמִי, אָבֹא אֵלֶיךָ וּבֵרַכְתִּיךָ.

ז. רַבִּי אֶלְעָזָר אִישׁ בַּרְתּוֹתָא אוֹמֵר: תֶּן לוֹ מִשֶּׁלּוֹ, שֶׁאַתָּה וְשֶׁלָּךְ
שֶׁלּוֹ. וְכֵן בְּדָוִד הוּא אוֹמֵר: כִּי מִמְּךָ הַכֹּל וּמִיָּדְךָ נָתַנּוּ לָךְ.

רַבִּי יַעֲקֹב אוֹמֵר: הַמְהַלֵּךְ בַּדֶּרֶךְ וְשׁוֹנֶה, וּמַפְסִיק מִמִּשְׁנָתוֹ וְאוֹמֵר:

---

ferior to that of five, since five unites four distinct directions, while three unites only two (*Maharal*).

Three...judges. A Jewish court comprises no less than three judges (*Rambam*).

You mention My Name. Translation of *azkir* as "*you* mention" follows *Ritva* and *Sforno*.

7. Give of...that which is His. Do not be stingy when giving charity, since you are not giving away your own possessions, but those of G-d, who has entrusted them with you for this purpose (*Meiri*). And be humble, since the fact that you *own* money to give away—and that you have the free choice to do so (*Avodat Yisrael*)—is a gift from G-d (*Biurim*).

You...are His. Realize that your entire existence is dependent upon G-d; that you and all of your reality would be nonexistent without Him. You will then be more willing to sacrifice your own comforts and desires for the sake of G-dly ideals (see *Midrash Shmuel*).

So did David say. David said this in reference to the funds donated toward the construction of the Holy Temple in Jerusalem.

One who walks . . .

NATURE AND TORAH. Judaism encourages the appreciation of nature and even mandates the recitation of a special blessing when seeing beautiful sights. For in the beauty of nature, we are offered a glimpse into G-d's greatness.

But there is a higher window through which we can gain an even deeper appreciation of Divinity—the window of Torah.

Torah is inherently transcendent from the world. It therefore transports its student from the limited perception of the physical world to a loftier appreciation of Divinity than is achieved through viewing the beauty of nature.

One who is studying Torah should therefore not interrupt his study, even to marvel at the beauty of G-d's physical world.

● The first part of the Mishnah

6. R. Chalafta ben Dosa the man of the village of Chananya said: If ten people sit together and occupy themselves with Torah, the Divine Presence rests among them, as it says: *G-d stands in the assembly of G-d.*[8] How do we know that the same is true even of five? For it is stated: *[He builds His strata in the Heavens]; His band He has founded upon the earth.*[9] How do we know that the same is true even of three? For it is stated: *He renders judgment among the judges.*[10] How do we know that the same is true even of two? For it is stated: *Then the G-d-fearing conversed, a man with his fellow, and G-d listened and heard.*[11] How do we know that the same is true even of one? For it is stated: *In every place where you mention My Name I will come to you and bless you.*[12]

7. R. Elazar man of Bartota said: Give to Him of what is His, for you and what is yours are His. And so did David say: *For all things are from You, and from Your own have we given You.*[13]

R. Yaakov said: One who walks on the road and studies [Torah], and interrupts his study and remarks, "How beautiful is this tree!

---

6. The Divine Presence. When even one person studies Torah, the Divine presence rests upon him. But when people study together, the level of Divine presence is increased. So *two* people studying elicit a greater degree of Divine presence than one person; *three* more than two; *five* more than three or four; *ten* and above more than five, six, seven, eight or nine (*Maharal, Midrash Shmuel*).

Ten. Ten is the only number that is a complete unit. No number is greater than ten. After ten, we return to one. (Eleven is in reality 10+1.) Any number beneath ten is considered deficient, since additional numbers can be added to it. An assembly of ten therefore reflects G-d's completeness and creates the greatest receptacle for His presence (*Maharal*). (In Torah, *assembly* refers to a group of ten, see *Megillah* 23b.)

Five. While not as complete a number as ten, five embodies unity and therefore reflects G-d's unity. *Four* embodies polarity and division, such as the four directions, which are separate and disunited. *Five* embodies unity, since the fifth element, the center, brings unity, a common point, to the four diverse directions (*Maharal*).

Three. Three contains the diversity of two along with a third element that unites them. It is therefore considered a unified number, paralleling the unity of G-d. Its unity, however, is in-

---

8. Psalms 82:1.   9. Amos 9:6.   10. Psalms 82:1.   11. Malachi 3:16.   12. Exodus 20:21.
13. I Chronicles 29:14.

מַה נָּאֶה אִילָן זֶה, מַה נָּאֶה נִיר זֶה, מַעֲלֶה עָלָיו הַכָּתוּב כְּאִלּוּ מִתְחַיֵּב בְּנַפְשׁוֹ.

ח. רַבִּי דוֹסְתָּאִי בְּרַבִּי יַנַּאי מִשּׁוּם רַבִּי מֵאִיר אוֹמֵר: כָּל הַשּׁוֹכֵחַ דָּבָר אֶחָד מִמִּשְׁנָתוֹ, מַעֲלֶה עָלָיו הַכָּתוּב כְּאִלּוּ מִתְחַיֵּב בְּנַפְשׁוֹ, שֶׁנֶּאֱמַר: רַק הִשָּׁמֶר לְךָ וּשְׁמֹר נַפְשְׁךָ מְאֹד פֶּן תִּשְׁכַּח אֶת הַדְּבָרִים אֲשֶׁר רָאוּ עֵינֶיךָ. יָכוֹל אֲפִילוּ תָּקְפָה עָלָיו מִשְׁנָתוֹ, תַּלְמוּד לוֹמַר: וּפֶן יָסוּרוּ מִלְּבָבְךָ כֹּל יְמֵי חַיֶּיךָ, הָא אֵינוֹ מִתְחַיֵּב בְּנַפְשׁוֹ עַד שֶׁיֵּשֵׁב וִיסִירֵם מִלִּבּוֹ.

ט. רַבִּי חֲנִינָא בֶּן דּוֹסָא אוֹמֵר: כֹּל שֶׁיִּרְאַת חֶטְאוֹ קוֹדֶמֶת לְחָכְמָתוֹ, חָכְמָתוֹ מִתְקַיֶּמֶת. וְכֹל שֶׁחָכְמָתוֹ קוֹדֶמֶת לְיִרְאַת חֶטְאוֹ, אֵין חָכְמָתוֹ מִתְקַיֶּמֶת.

י. הוּא הָיָה אוֹמֵר: כֹּל שֶׁמַּעֲשָׂיו מְרֻבִּין מֵחָכְמָתוֹ, חָכְמָתוֹ מִתְקַיֶּמֶת. וְכֹל שֶׁחָכְמָתוֹ מְרֻבָּה מִמַּעֲשָׂיו, אֵין חָכְמָתוֹ מִתְקַיֶּמֶת. הוּא הָיָה אוֹמֵר: כֹּל שֶׁרוּחַ הַבְּרִיּוֹת נוֹחָה הֵימֶנּוּ, רוּחַ הַמָּקוֹם נוֹחָה הֵימֶנּוּ.

Guard your soul so that *you should not forget* (*Meam Loez*).

Too difficult. This refers to one who forgets a complex thought because he never fully understood it (*R. Moshe Alashkar*).

9. Fear of sin precedes his wisdom. If one values his knowledge more than the purity of his character he will ultimately lose his knowledge as well and remain without either (*Midrash Shmuel*).

● "Fear of sin," in its ultimate sense, is the supra-rational devotion of the soul to G-d's will. This devotion is experienced during meditative prayer. "Wisdom," by contrast, refers to study of Torah with the *rational* mind.

In order for the wisdom to be enduring and have its proper effect it must be preceded by and imbued with the supra-rational experience of prayer (see *Biurim*).

10. Good deeds exceed his wisdom. By purifying his soul through good deeds, he makes himself a vessel for the otherworldly wisdom of Torah, which would otherwise escape him (*Maharal*).

Ramban writes in his famous letter to his son: "At the end of every study session, examine what you have learned and see if there is something that you can apply in practice."

G-d finds pleasing. To love G-d—or to imagine that one loves G-d—is not necessarily an expression of self-lessness. Self-centeredness and spiritual seeking are not mutually exclusive—they often come together. The true path to G-d requires transcendence of self. If you truly love G-d, you will love His children—and

How beautiful is this plowed field!" Scripture considers it as if he bears guilt for [the loss of] his life.

8. R. Dosta'ey bar Yannai said in the name of R. Meir: Whoever forgets anything of his Torah learning, Scripture considers it as if he bears guilt for his soul, for it is stated: *But beware and guard your soul well lest you forget the things that your eyes have seen.*[14] It might have been thought that this applies even if [he forgot because] the subject matter was too difficult for him. Scripture therefore adds: *And lest they be removed from your heart all the days of your life*[14]—a person does not bear guilt for his soul until he sits [idly] and removes them [through lack of diligence in reviewing his studies].

9. R. Chanina ben Dosa said: Anyone whose fear of sin precedes his wisdom, his wisdom will endure; but anyone whose wisdom precedes his fear of sin, his wisdom will not endure.

10. He used to say: Anyone whose [good] deeds exceed his wisdom, his wisdom will endure; but anyone whose wisdom exceeds his [good] deeds, his wisdom will not endure. He used to say: Anyone who the spirit of people finds pleasing, the spirit of G-d finds pleasing; but anyone who the spirit of people does not

---

speaks of our service of G-d in the mundane arena of life—giving charity from our physical possessions. In the second part, the Mishnah speaks of serving G-d through transcendence from the physical, through the study of Torah (*Biurim*).

Bears guilt for his life. A person who is on the pious level of Avot—beyond the letter of the law—is held to a higher standard. Hence this severe pronouncement for his seemingly minor infraction (*Biurim*).

8. How can one be held accountable for forgetting? According to early commentators, one who forgets has

obviously not reviewed properly. According to later commentators, one is held accountable for failing to study in a way that precludes forgetting to begin with (see below).

Forgets. The act of forgetting itself is a negative occurrence, since one forfeits the life-force contained in the forgotten Torah thought. Every Torah thought should be so firmly embedded in one's being that it should be impossible to forget (*Biurim*).

Guard your soul. If a person does not guard his soul from materialistic overindulgence, the Torah knowledge that he has will escape him. Hence:

---

14. Deuteronomy 4:9.

וְכֹל שֶׁאֵין רוּחַ הַבְּרִיוֹת נוֹחָה הֵימֶנּוּ, אֵין רוּחַ הַמָּקוֹם נוֹחָה הֵימֶנּוּ.

רַבִּי דוֹסָא בֶּן הָרְכִּינַס אוֹמֵר: שֵׁנָה שֶׁל שַׁחֲרִית, וְיַיִן שֶׁל צָהֳרַיִם, וְשִׂיחַת הַיְלָדִים, וִישִׁיבַת בָּתֵּי כְנֵסִיּוֹת שֶׁל עַמֵּי הָאָרֶץ, מוֹצִיאִין אֶת הָאָדָם מִן הָעוֹלָם.

יא. רַבִּי אֶלְעָזָר הַמּוֹדָעִי אוֹמֵר: הַמְחַלֵּל אֶת הַקֳּדָשִׁים, וְהַמְבַזֶּה אֶת הַמּוֹעֲדוֹת, וְהַמַּלְבִּין פְּנֵי חֲבֵרוֹ בָּרַבִּים, וְהַמֵּפֵר בְּרִיתוֹ שֶׁל אַבְרָהָם אָבִינוּ, וְהַמְגַלֶּה פָנִים בַּתּוֹרָה שֶׁלֹּא כַהֲלָכָה, אַף עַל פִּי שֶׁיֵּשׁ בְּיָדוֹ תּוֹרָה וּמַעֲשִׂים טוֹבִים, אֵין לוֹ חֵלֶק לָעוֹלָם הַבָּא.

יב. רַבִּי יִשְׁמָעֵאל אוֹמֵר: הֱוֵי קַל לְרֹאשׁ, וְנוֹחַ לְתִשְׁחוֹרֶת, וֶהֱוֵי מְקַבֵּל אֶת כָּל הָאָדָם בְּשִׂמְחָה.

---

festivals are fixed according to the days of the months, the first day of which is established and sanctified by man (the Rabbinic court). The festivals are an example from the realm of **time**.

Whitens: He humiliates a *friend*—not just a stranger—a person with whom he has created a relationship, a sacred reality, since he denies man's ability to sanctify a human relationship. Humiliation is an example from the realm of **human relationships**.

Abraham's Covenant: Circumcision is called "the covenant of Abraham" because Abraham bequeathed to his descendants the spiritual power to enter G-d's eternal covenant through circumcision. Circumcision, then, is a holy covenant that is facilitated by a human being, Abraham. The covenant is an example from the realm of the **body**.

Interprets...contrary: Distorting Torah and misinterpreting it in a way that contradicts *halachah* requires the type of Torah scholarship that one would receive from a teacher, a fellow human.

This individual mocks what he has gained from his fellow—since nothing gained from another human is sacred to him—and uses it to misinterpret Torah. Misinterpreting Torah is an example from the realm of the **mind and soul** (*Biurim*).

The World to Come: Unlike other sins, which can be erased through punishment, denial of fundamental Torah principles—such as man's ability to sanctify his world—cannot be undone with any penalty and the individual is therefore unable to experience the World to Come (*Biurim;* see *Sanhedrin* 10:1).

12. In the presence of a true leader, be acquiescent. Leave your pride and self-importance behind. But when in the presence of the young—the black-haired (*tishchoret*)—remain composed; Do not be playful and lighthearted with them. On the other hand, do not think that because you cannot be playful with them you must greet them sternly. Not so:

Receive every person "small or great,

find pleasing, the spirit of G-d does not find pleasing.

R. Dosa ben Harkinas said: The sleep of the [late] morning, wine at midday, children's conversation, and sitting in the gathering places of the ignorant, drive a man from the world.

11. R. Elazar of Modi'in said: One who profanes sacred things, one who degrades the festivals, one who whitens the face of his friend in public, one who abrogates the covenant of our father Abraham [circumcision], and one who interprets the Torah in a manner contrary to its true intent—even if he has Torah and good deeds in his hand—has no share in the World to Come.

12. R. Yishmael said: Be submissive in the presence of a [righteous] leader, pleasant (and composed) with a young person, and receive every person with joy.

---

they will love you (see *Yalkut Yehuda* in *Likkutei Battar Likkutei*).

G-d does not find pleasing. If the Mishnah would not repeat itself in this way one might have concluded that a person who is not liked by people may or may not be liked by G-d. The Mishnah therefore repeats itself in the reverse to emphasize that if one is disliked by people he is disliked by G-d (*Midrash Shmuel*).

Drive a man from the world. The Torah cannot find an enduring home in one who engages in idle activity. Such a person is driven from the world, since he loses his connection to Torah, which is the source of true life (*Maharal*).

11. This individual worships the intellect and disdains the physical. He therefore desecrates sacred objects, since he cannot fathom the idea of physical objects being sacred; he degrades the festivals, since they are celebrated with physical feasting; he embarrasses his friend, since human beings are physical; he abrogates the covenant of Abraham, since he cannot fathom the idea of a lowly organ possessing G-d's covenant; and he misinterprets Torah by turning even the clearly literal portions of the Torah into metaphor, since he does not believe that G-d has any care for physical deeds (*Maharal*).

● Alternatively, this individual, though believing that G-d can sanctify the physical, refuses to recognize the ability of *a human* to sanctify the physical. In each of the Mishnah's five cases the individual is belittling the holiness created by a human being.

The Mishnah uses five examples corresponding to five realms within man's experience:

Sacred Objects: Physical matter is, on the most part, sanctified by human beings; the character described in this Mishnah therefore denies their holiness. This serves an example of his derision in the realm of **matter**.

Festivals: The festivals, unlike Shabbat, are sanctified by man, since the

יג. רַבִּי עֲקִיבָא אוֹמֵר: שְׂחוֹק וְקַלּוּת רֹאשׁ, מַרְגִּילִין אֶת הָאָדָם לְעֶרְוָה. מַסֹרֶת סְיָג לַתּוֹרָה, מַעְשְׂרוֹת סְיָג לָעֹשֶׁר, נְדָרִים סְיָג לִפְרִישׁוּת, סְיָג לַחָכְמָה שְׁתִיקָה.

יד. הוּא הָיָה אוֹמֵר: חָבִיב אָדָם שֶׁנִּבְרָא בְצֶלֶם, חִבָּה יְתֵרָה נוֹדַעַת לוֹ שֶׁנִּבְרָא בְצֶלֶם, שֶׁנֶּאֱמַר: כִּי בְּצֶלֶם אֱלֹהִים עָשָׂה אֶת הָאָדָם. חֲבִיבִין יִשְׂרָאֵל שֶׁנִּקְרְאוּ בָנִים לַמָּקוֹם, חִבָּה יְתֵרָה נוֹדַעַת לָהֶם שֶׁנִּקְרְאוּ בָנִים לַמָּקוֹם, שֶׁנֶּאֱמַר: בָּנִים אַתֶּם לַייָ אֱלֹהֵיכֶם. חֲבִיבִין יִשְׂרָאֵל שֶׁנִּתַּן לָהֶם כְּלִי חֶמְדָּה, חִבָּה יְתֵרָה נוֹדַעַת לָהֶם שֶׁנִּתַּן לָהֶם כְּלִי חֶמְדָּה, שֶׁנֶּאֱמַר: כִּי לֶקַח טוֹב נָתַתִּי לָכֶם, תּוֹרָתִי אַל תַּעֲזֹבוּ.

טו. הַכֹּל צָפוּי, וְהָרְשׁוּת נְתוּנָה, וּבְטוֹב הָעוֹלָם נִדּוֹן, וְהַכֹּל לְפִי רֹב הַמַּעֲשֶׂה.

---

not value the recipient of his favor he does not care to inform him of it. The fact that G-d informs man of this quality is an additional expression of Divine love (*Rambam*).

15. Everything is foreseen. Although G-d foresees that a person is about to act foolishly, He does not interfere and "choice is given." (*Maharal*).

Choice is given. Because G-d fills all time and space, man would naturally be incapable of doing *anything*, let alone that which contradicts the Divine will. G-d actively *empowers* man with the "unnatural" ability to act, even immorally.

A person should ponder the fact that G-d Himself has *given* him freedom of choice so that he can willingly make the right choice. He will then fulfill that mandate with joy, love, and devotion (*Biurim*).

With goodness. Even though "all is seen" and a person is constantly in the King's presence, he is not judged by that standard (*Biurim*).

Even when G-d *judges* the world it is an expression of goodness; i.e., it is for the positive purpose of cleansing the evildoer (*Tiferet Yisrael*).

Preponderance. A person is judged according to the *majority* of his deeds. If they are primarily righteous he is judged favorably, etc. (*Rashi*).

● FREEDOM OF CHOICE VS. G-D'S OMNISCIENCE. Just as a stargazer's prediction does not cause an event to occur, so, too G-d's foreknowledge of man's decision does not influence that decision (*Raavad's* gloss on *Rambam*, Laws of *Teshuvah* 5:4). Man's decision influences G-d's knowledge.

G-d is beyond time. His knowledge of a "future" event is similar to human knowledge of a past event, which has no bearing on the event (*Sforno, Midrash Shmuel*). He knows things because they have already happened. Obviously, the idea of "be-

13. R. Akiva said: Laughter and frivolity accustom a man to lewdness. The tradition is a [protective] fence for Torah; tithes are a fence for riches; vows are a fence for abstinence; a fence for wisdom is silence.

14. He used to say: Beloved is man, for he was created in the [Divine] image; it is [an expression of] even a greater love that it was made known to him that he was created in the [Divine] image, as it says: *For in the image of G-d He made man.*[15] Beloved are the people Israel, for they are called children of G-d; it is [an expression of] even a greater love that it was made known to them that they are called children of G-d, as it says: *You are the children of G-d Your G-d.*[16] Beloved are the people Israel, for a precious article was given to them; it is even a greater love that it was made known to them that they were given a precious article, as it says: *A good Teaching have I given you; My Torah, do not forsake.*[17]

15. Everything is foreseen, yet freedom of choice is given; the world is judged with goodness, and everything is according to the preponderance of [good] deeds.

---

free or enslaved, indeed, any member of the human species—with joy" (*Rambam*).

13. R. Akiva qualifies the statement of R. Yishmael: Greet every person with joy—but do not get carried away to the point of frivolity, which leads to impurity. He then lists a number of behaviors that lead to holiness, the opposite of impurity (*Maharal*).

Tradition. This refers to the oral tradition through which we determine the meaning of the verses of the Written Torah and its laws (*Rashi*).

Tithes. Generously giving charity causes one to receive additional wealth from G-d (*Rashi, R. Yonah*).

Vows. When a person takes vows and keeps them he acquires self-discipline and the ability to control his impulses when challenged with destructive temptations (*Rambam*).

Silence. One who is more concerned with expressing his own view than hearing those of the masters will not gain true wisdom (*R. Yonah*).

14. In the image. Unlike animals, human beings walk upright, a symbol of their sovereignty over all of creation. This upright stature mirrors the sovereignty of G-d, above Whom there is none (*Maharal*). The image of G-d refers also to human intelligence and freedom of choice (*Mefarshim*).

Made known. When a person does

---

15. Genesis 9:6.   16. Deuteronomy 14:1.   17. Proverbs 4:2.

טז. הוּא הָיָה אוֹמֵר: הַכֹּל נָתוּן בָּעֵרָבוֹן, וּמְצוּדָה פְרוּסָה עַל כָּל הַחַיִּים, הֶחָנוּת פְּתוּחָה, וְהַחֶנְוָנִי מַקִּיף, וְהַפִּנְקָס פָּתוּחַ, וְהַיָּד כּוֹתֶבֶת, וְכָל הָרוֹצֶה לִלְווֹת יָבֹא וְיִלְוֶה, וְהַגַּבָּאִין מַחֲזִירִין תָּדִיר בְּכָל יוֹם, וְנִפְרָעִין מִן הָאָדָם מִדַּעְתּוֹ וְשֶׁלֹּא מִדַּעְתּוֹ, וְיֵשׁ לָהֶם עַל מַה שֶׁיִּסְמֹכוּ, וְהַדִּין דִּין אֱמֶת, וְהַכֹּל מְתֻקָּן לִסְעוּדָה.

יז. רַבִּי אֶלְעָזָר בֶּן עֲזַרְיָה אוֹמֵר: אִם אֵין תּוֹרָה אֵין דֶּרֶךְ אֶרֶץ, אִם אֵין דֶּרֶךְ אֶרֶץ אֵין תּוֹרָה, אִם אֵין חָכְמָה אֵין יִרְאָה, אִם אֵין

---

death of his sheep is equal to the rich man's suffering at the death of his ox (*Sforno*).

For the feast. The sole purpose of all the above is to prepare for the feast: the life of the World to Come (*Rambam, R. Yonah*). The purpose of punishment is not Divine revenge, G-d forbid, but to purify the person so that he may enjoy the Divine splendor in the World to Come (*Meam Loez*).

17. Without Torah there is no social decorum (*derech eretz*). Social decorum that lacks a Divine foundation and is based solely on human intellect ultimately deteriorates and fails (*Maharal*).

● *HaChasid* translates *derech eretz* as "the way of the land." He interprets the phrase to mean that if not for the Torah, the world and all of its customs—*the way of the land*—would not exist, since the world was created to serve as a platform for the fulfillment of Torah.

Without social decorum (*derech eretz*) there is no Torah. The Torah does not rest within a person who lacks fine character traits (*R. Yonah*).

● *HaChasid* interprets the phrase to mean that if human beings were not earthly as they are—*derech eretz, the way of the land*—they would not have received the Torah: it would have remained with the angels.

Without wisdom there is no awe. When a person is close to and aware of the king, he is awed; not so one who is distant. Wisdom brings one close to the King (*Maharal*).

Without awe there is no wisdom. The purpose of wisdom is to attain awe of Heaven. Wisdom that does not result in awe will not endure, since no entity can exist unless it attains its purpose and fulfillment (*Maharal*).

Without knowledge there is no understanding. If one does not possess knowledge it is because he did not toil with the power of understanding to attain it (*Sforno*).

Without understanding there is no knowledge. Understanding refers to the *process* of defining the essence of a thing, to see past its external form to its inner being. Without this process

16. He used to say: Everything is given on collateral and a net is spread over all the living; the shop is open and the Shopkeeper extends credit, the ledger is open and the hand writes, and whoever wishes to borrow, let him come and borrow; the collectors make their rounds regularly, each day, they exact payment from man with or without his knowledge, and they have on what to rely; the judgment is a judgment of truth; and everything is prepared for the feast.

17. R. Elazar ben Azaryah said: Without Torah, there is no social decorum; without social decorum, there is no Torah. Without wisdom, there is no awe; without awe, there is no wisdom. Without knowledge, there is no understanding; without understanding,

---

yond time" cannot be fully grasped by human intelligence.

See *Ohr Samayach* on *Rambam*, Laws of *Teshuvah* 5:4 for an outline of the various solutions offered by Jewish philosophers (*Igrot Kodesh* 3:40). See also *Biurim* (*hosafot michtavim*).

16. Everything is given on collateral. Everything that a person possesses—life, talents, possessions, social position—is given to him by G-d on collateral. He should therefore "return" these loans by using them for their intended purpose—to make the world a better place. If he uses them for egotistical and materialistic purposes, he will ultimately have to pay in some form (see *Kol Sofer, Midrash Shmuel*).

A net is spread. It is impossible to escape the day of death and judgment (*Rashi*).

The shop is open. An open store invites people to enter and take whatever their hearts desire without thought of repaying. Similarly, mor-

tals see the world as an open shop. They do not consider a day when they will have to repay the Shopkeeper (*R. Yonah*).

Credit. G-d does not repay man immediately for his misdeeds (*Mefarshim*); He gives him time, waiting for him to repent (*Midrash David*).

The collectors. I.e., forms of punishment (*Mefarshim*).

With or without his knowledge. When a person suffers and knows the purpose of his suffering, his suffering is eased. But when a person is oblivious to the misdeeds that caused this suffering, he suffers much greater pain and angst (*R. Yonah*).

They have on what to rely. Those who have "borrowed" and "partaken of the open store" have on what to rely: they can repent (*Meiri*).

Judgment of truth. Each person is punished according to his situation: the suffering of the poor man at the

יִרְאָה אֵין חָכְמָה, אִם אֵין דַּעַת אֵין בִּינָה, אִם אֵין בִּינָה אֵין
דַּעַת, אִם אֵין קֶמַח אֵין תּוֹרָה, אִם אֵין תּוֹרָה אֵין קֶמַח.

הוּא הָיָה אוֹמֵר: כֹּל שֶׁחָכְמָתוֹ מְרֻבָּה מִמַּעֲשָׂיו, לְמָה הוּא דוֹמֶה:
לְאִילָן שֶׁעֲנָפָיו מְרֻבִּין וְשָׁרָשָׁיו מוּעָטִין, וְהָרוּחַ בָּאָה וְעוֹקַרְתּוֹ
וְהוֹפַכְתּוֹ עַל פָּנָיו, שֶׁנֶּאֱמַר: וְהָיָה כְּעַרְעָר בָּעֲרָבָה, וְלֹא יִרְאֶה כִּי
יָבֹא טוֹב, וְשָׁכַן חֲרֵרִים בַּמִּדְבָּר, אֶרֶץ מְלֵחָה וְלֹא תֵשֵׁב. אֲבָל, כֹּל
שֶׁמַּעֲשָׂיו מְרֻבִּין מֵחָכְמָתוֹ, לְמָה הוּא דוֹמֶה: לְאִילָן שֶׁעֲנָפָיו
מוּעָטִין וְשָׁרָשָׁיו מְרֻבִּין, שֶׁאֲפִילוּ כָּל הָרוּחוֹת שֶׁבָּעוֹלָם בָּאוֹת
וְנוֹשְׁבוֹת בּוֹ, אֵין מְזִיזִין אוֹתוֹ מִמְּקוֹמוֹ, שֶׁנֶּאֱמַר: וְהָיָה כְּעֵץ
שָׁתוּל עַל מַיִם, וְעַל יוּבַל יְשַׁלַּח שָׁרָשָׁיו, וְלֹא יִרְאֶה כִּי יָבֹא חֹם,
וְהָיָה עָלֵהוּ רַעֲנָן, וּבִשְׁנַת בַּצֹּרֶת לֹא יִדְאָג, וְלֹא יָמִישׁ מֵעֲשׂוֹת
פֶּרִי.

יח. רַבִּי אֱלִיעֶזֶר (בֶּן) חִסְמָא אוֹמֵר: קִנִּין וּפִתְחֵי נִדָּה, הֵן הֵן גּוּפֵי

---

dimension with fortitude and infinite potential (*Biurim*; see also *Midrash Shmuel*).

Wisdom exceeds his deeds. This individual studies Torah and seeks wisdom for selfish purposes. He *"trusts in man"*—and studies in order to gain the admiration of others (*Midrash Shmuel*).

Whose branches are numerous. The branches not only do not keep the tree grounded, they cause the tree to be uprooted by trapping the wind. Similarly, wisdom that lacks the proper context can ruin a person (*Ha-Chasid*). Cf. below 4:5, "Exploits."

18. This Mishnah declares the superiority of the Divine Torah over the natural sciences. The laws of Torah provide a path toward spiritual per-

fection (the word *halachah* means *path*), while the natural sciences leave man without direction. They are like condiments: complements to a meal but incapable of sustaining the soul (*Maharal*).

Bird sacrifices. This refers to the complex calculations that must be made when two types of bird offerings are accidentally mixed and whose identities become unknown (*Bartenura*).

Bird-sacrifices and . . . menstruation. R. Eliezer chooses these laws for a number of reasons:
1) They require mathematical calculations, and can therefore be compared to astronomy and geometry.
2) They are cases where doubt arises and the *halachah* provides a clear path to the proper way. The sci-

there is no knowledge. Without flour [sustenance], there is no Torah; without Torah, there is no flour.

He used to say: Anyone whose wisdom exceeds his [good] deeds, to what can he be compared? To a tree whose branches are numerous but whose roots are few, and the wind comes and uproots it and turns it upside down; as it says: *[Cursed is the man who trusts in man... and turns his heart from G-d.] He shall be like a lonely tree on the flatland and shall not see when good comes; he shall dwell parched in the desert, on land salty and unsettled.*[18] But anyone whose [good] deeds exceed his wisdom, to what can he be compared? To a tree whose branches are few but whose roots are numerous, so that even if all the winds in the world were to come and blow against it, they could not move it from its place; as it says: *[Blessed is the man who trusts in G-d....] He shall be like a tree planted by waters, toward the stream spreading its roots, and it shall not feel when the heat comes, and its foliage shall be verdant; in the year of drought it shall not worry, nor shall it cease from yielding fruit.*[19]

18. R. Eliezer (son of) Chisma said: The laws pertaining to bird-sacrifices and the calculation of the onset of menstruation—these

---

there is no true knowledge, only superficial knowledge (*Sforno*).

Without flour there is no Torah. Without food, one cannot study Torah (*Bartenura*).

Without Torah there is no flour. If the entire world would devote itself to material pursuits and abandon Torah, the world would cease to exist (*Midrash Shmuel* citing R. Yisrael).

Alternatively, if he does not procure his livelihood in a manner consistent with Torah, his earnings are not pure like flour, but tainted like coarse chaff (*Maamarei Admur Hazaken, Bereishit* 45).

● WISDOM AND DEED. Man serves G-d in two ways: like a student, through the wisdom of intellect, and like a son, through supra-rational devotion, which is expressed in deed. The deed aspect is an expression of the essence of the soul, which remains aloof from the body and therefore transcends intellect. The intellectual dimension stems from the part of the soul that dwells within the body and human consciousness. Wisdom is therefore called a *branch* of the soul's *root* (see *Sanhedrin* 110b).

The deed aspect must be primary. It must be the foundation upon which the intellectual dimension is built. It then imbues the intellectual

---

18. Jeremiah 17:6.   19. Ibid. 17:8.

הֲלָכוֹת. תְּקוּפוֹת וְגִמַּטְרִיָאוֹת, פַּרְפְּרָאוֹת לַחָכְמָה.

רַבִּי חֲנַנְיָא בֶּן עֲקַשְׁיָא אוֹמֵר: רָצָה הַקָּדוֹשׁ בָּרוּךְ הוּא לְזַכּוֹת אֶת יִשְׂרָאֵל, לְפִיכָךְ הִרְבָּה לָהֶם תּוֹרָה וּמִצְוֹת, שֶׁנֶּאֱמַר: יְיָ חָפֵץ לְמַעַן צִדְקוֹ, יַגְדִּיל תּוֹרָה וְיַאְדִּיר.

Gematriya'ot. I.e., geometry (*Meiri, Maharal*). Alternatively, this refers to the art of *gematria*, the interpretation of Torah based on the numeric equivalents of its letters and words (*Lechem Shamayim*).

● R. Eliezer himself was an expert mathematician. The Talmud relates that he was capable of estimating the amount of drops in the sea (*Horayot* 10a). Being an expert in both Torah and mathematics, R. Eliezer was in the position to compare the two (*Tosfot Yom Tov*).

46

are essentials of *halachah* [Torah law]; the calculation of cycles [astronomy] and *gematriya'ot* are condiments to wisdom.

Rabbi Chananyah ben Akashya said: The Holy One, blessed be He, wished to make Israel meritorious. He therefore increased for them Torah and mitzvot, as it says: *G-d desired, for the sake of his [Israel's] righteousness, to make the Torah great and glorious.*[20] (*Makkot* 3:16)

---

ences, by contrast, do not offer any direction on life's moral questions and doubts (*Maharal*).

3) They are examples of Torah law that deal with seemingly lowly matters. R. Eliezer thereby to em-

phasizes that Torah law, regardless of the subject, is genuinely lofty because of its Divine source. Other sciences, lofty as they seem, are limited to the realm of nature and created reality (*Abarbanel*).

---

20. Isaiah 42:21.

פֶּרֶק רְבִיעִי

כָּל יִשְׂרָאֵל יֵשׁ לָהֶם חֵלֶק לְעוֹלָם הַבָּא, שֶׁנֶּאֱמַר: וְעַמֵּךְ כֻּלָּם צַדִּיקִים, לְעוֹלָם יִירְשׁוּ אָרֶץ, נֵצֶר מַטָּעַי מַעֲשֵׂה יָדַי לְהִתְפָּאֵר.

א. בֶּן זוֹמָא אוֹמֵר: אֵיזֶהוּ חָכָם, הַלּוֹמֵד מִכָּל אָדָם, שֶׁנֶּאֱמַר: מִכָּל מְלַמְּדַי הִשְׂכַּלְתִּי, כִּי עֵדְוֹתֶיךָ שִׂיחָה לִי.

אֵיזֶהוּ גִבּוֹר, הַכּוֹבֵשׁ אֶת יִצְרוֹ, שֶׁנֶּאֱמַר: טוֹב אֶרֶךְ אַפַּיִם מִגִּבּוֹר, וּמוֹשֵׁל בְּרוּחוֹ מִלֹּכֵד עִיר.

אֵיזֶהוּ עָשִׁיר, הַשָּׂמֵחַ בְּחֶלְקוֹ, שֶׁנֶּאֱמַר: יְגִיעַ כַּפֶּיךָ כִּי תֹאכֵל, אַשְׁרֶיךָ וְטוֹב לָךְ, אַשְׁרֶיךָ בָּעוֹלָם הַזֶּה, וְטוֹב לָךְ לָעוֹלָם הַבָּא.

אֵיזֶהוּ מְכֻבָּד, הַמְכַבֵּד אֶת הַבְּרִיּוֹת, שֶׁנֶּאֱמַר: כִּי מְכַבְּדַי אֲכַבֵּד וּבֹזַי יֵקָלּוּ.

ב. בֶּן עַזַּאי אוֹמֵר: הֱוֵי רָץ לְמִצְוָה קַלָּה, וּבוֹרֵחַ מִן הָעֲבֵרָה, שֶׁמִּצְוָה

He who is slow to anger...masters his passions.... Self-control and the ability to forgive is a greater strength than fearless bravery (*R. Yonah*). *Bartenura* interprets the verse as follows: "Patience that is borne of the strength of self-control (*mi'gibor*) is good"—as opposed to patience borne of a feeble disposition.

He who honors the creatures. A "creature" is the type of person whose only redeeming factor is that he is G-d's creation (see *Tanya* ch. 32 and above 1:12). The ability to honor even such a person is derived from the following verse:

...Those who despise Me shall be despised. One who despises any of G-d's creatures is as if he despises G-d Himself, G-d forbid. As the homely person said to the sage who had mocked his appearance, "Go to the Craftsman Who made me" (*Taanit* 20b). One who looks down upon G-d's creatures despises G-d and will be looked down upon; but one who honors G-d's creatures honors G-d Himself and will be honored (*Biurim*).

2. Ben Azzai speaks not only of physical running—which is not appropriate in for many *mitzvot*—but of an emotional yearning and joy in the fulfillment of a mitzvah, even a "minor" mitzvah. This pleasure and joy stems from awareness that a mitzvah, even minor, connects one with the Infinite One. Yet even a person who has not reached this level should run to do a mitzvah, since the act of running will bring him closer to running instinctively (*Biurim*; see *Chinuch*, 15).

CHAPTER FOUR

All of Israel have a share in the World to Come, as it says, *Your people are all righteous; they will inherit the Land forever; they are the branch of My planting, the work of My hands in which I take pride.*[1] (Sanhedrin 11:1)

1. Ben Zoma said: Who is wise? He who learns from every person, as it says: *From all those who have taught me I have gained wisdom; Your testimonies are my conversation.*[2]

    Who is strong? He who subdues his inclination, as it says: *He who is slow to anger is better than the strong man, and he who masters his passions is better than one who conquers a city.*[3]

    Who is rich? He who is happy with his lot, as it says: *When you eat of the labor of your hands, happy are you and it shall be well with you.*[4] *Happy are you*—in this world; *and it shall be well with you*—in the World to Come.

    Who is honored? He who honors the creatures, as it says: *Those who honor Me I will honor, and those who despise Me shall be degraded.*[5]

2. Ben Azzai said: Run to [perform even] a minor mitzvah, and flee from transgression; for a mitzvah leads to another mitzvah, and a

---

1. Wisdom, strength, wealth and honor gain meaning only when utilized for a higher purpose (see *Mefarshim*).

He who learns from every person. Even from those who are inferior to him. He thereby shows that his desire to learn is pure—"to know and perceive G-d" (*Tosfot Yom Tov*)—not for his own self-aggrandizement (*Bartenura*).

● One who knows all the wisdoms but does not love wisdom is not wise.

One who knows nothing but loves and pursues wisdom is called wise, since in the end he will attain wisdom and find the knowledge of G-d (*R. Yonah* citing the sages of the nations).

Your testimonies are my conversation. The Jewish people are a testimony to G-d's existence, as in the verse, '*You are My witnesses,*' says G-d (Isaiah 43:10). When a person sees his fellow as a testimony to G-d's existence, he can learn even from the seemingly least refined individual (*Biurim*).

---

1. Isaiah 60:21. 2. Psalms 119:99. 3. Proverbs 16:32. 4. Psalms 128:2. 5. I Samuel 2:30.

גּוֹרֶרֶת מִצְוָה, וַעֲבֵרָה גּוֹרֶרֶת עֲבֵרָה, שֶׁשְּׂכַר מִצְוָה מִצְוָה, וּשְׂכַר עֲבֵרָה עֲבֵרָה.

ג. הוּא הָיָה אוֹמֵר: אַל תְּהִי בָז לְכָל אָדָם וְאַל תְּהִי מַפְלִיג לְכָל דָּבָר, שֶׁאֵין לְךָ אָדָם שֶׁאֵין לוֹ שָׁעָה, וְאֵין לְךָ דָּבָר שֶׁאֵין לוֹ מָקוֹם.

ד. רַבִּי לְוִיטַס אִישׁ יַבְנֶה אוֹמֵר: מְאֹד מְאֹד הֱוֵי שְׁפַל רוּחַ, שֶׁתִּקְוַת אֱנוֹשׁ רִמָּה. רַבִּי יוֹחָנָן בֶּן בְּרוֹקָה אוֹמֵר: כָּל הַמְחַלֵּל שֵׁם שָׁמַיִם בַּסֵּתֶר, נִפְרָעִין מִמֶּנּוּ בַּגָּלוּי, אֶחָד שׁוֹגֵג וְאֶחָד מֵזִיד בְּחִלּוּל הַשֵּׁם.

ה. רַבִּי יִשְׁמָעֵאל בַּר רַבִּי יוֹסֵי אוֹמֵר: הַלּוֹמֵד תּוֹרָה עַל מְנָת לְלַמֵּד,

---

that a sin has been committed by a religious person, though it is not known by whom. For example, if ten religious individuals are in a home and one of them commits a crime, although the criminal's identity is not known, he desecrates G-d's Name since it becomes known that a religious person has committed a crime (*Maharal*).

• Whenever a person sins, even in private, he desecrates the Name of Heaven, i.e., the Divine presence that fills all of reality (*Avodat Yisrael*).

Meted out...in public. His private behavior will become public knowledge (*Rashi*). It is impossible for a person not to at some point betray his actions (*Avodat Yisrael; Kuntres Uma'ayan* p. 93).

Unintentionally. This refers to a person who sins privately and does not intend to desecrate G-d's Name. If his sin becomes public knowledge and thereby causes a desecration of

G-d's Name, the person will be punished publicly. This is not done to increase the person's punishment but rather for the sake of demonstrating to the world the severity of desecrating G-d's Name (*Sforno*).

The deliberate desecrator's punishment is obviously more severe (*Rambam*).

5. To teach. His goal in studying is to share the wisdom he will gain with others. G-d therefore grants him the ability to fulfill his goal (*Meiri*). His efforts in sharing the Torah will not compromise his own knowledge (*Midrash Shmuel*).

Not every student of Torah can teach it. Being a teacher requires a higher level of knowledge, one that provides the teacher with the answers he will inevitably be asked to give. Furthermore, in order to attract students, he must have a vast amount of knowledge. One who studies so that he can teach is granted a special blessing from Above that enhances his studies and knowledge (*Maharal*).

transgression leads to another transgression; for the reward of a mitzvah is a mitzvah, and the reward of a transgression is a transgression.

3. He used to say: Do not regard anyone with contempt, and do not reject any thing, for there is no man who does not have his hour and no thing that does not have its place.

4. R. Levitas man of Yavneh said: Be very, very humble, for the prospect of man is worms. R. Yochanan ben Berokah said: Whoever desecrates the Name of Heaven in secret, punishment will be meted out to him in public; unintentionally or intentionally, it is all the same in regard to the desecration of the Name.

5. R. Yishmael ben R. Yosay said: He who studies Torah in order to teach, is given the opportunity to study and to teach; and he who

---

The reward of a mitzvah is a mitzvah. The greatest reward for a mitzvah is a "mitzvah," meaning "bond," referring to the bond that is created between finite man and Infinite G-d through man's fulfillment of His will (see *HaChasid* and *Tanya* ch. 37).

The reward of a transgression is a transgression. There is no greater punishment for sin than sin itself—the fact that through sin one becomes separated and distant from the Creator (see *HaChasid*).

3. Every person and thing plays a role in the grand scheme of creation. Every person has his "hour," his moment in history to achieve his mission. And every thing has its "place," its function in the Divine plan (*Maharal*).

4. **Very, very.** Although generally one should not adopt the extreme in any characteristic, one should, however,

be exceedingly humble, even to the extent of eradicating every last shred of ego (*Rambam*).

Worms. Of course the soul will merit eternal life. R. Levitas is referring to the aspect of man that causes arrogance—the transient body (*Maharal*). See above 3:1.

Desecrates the Name of Heaven. The desecration of G-d's Name takes place primarily when one who is looked upon as a religious person acts improperly. He thereby degrades the Torah, since people say, "Look what happens when you study Torah. It is better not to study it at all." They may also say, "If such is the behavior of a 'man of G-d,' it must not be such a terrible thing" (*Maharal*).

In secret. I.e., in the presence of few people. Alternatively, the Mishnah refers to a case where it becomes known

51

מַסְפִּיקִין בְּיָדוֹ לִלְמוֹד וּלְלַמֵּד, וְהַלוֹמֵד עַל מְנָת לַעֲשׂוֹת, מַסְפִּיקִין בְּיָדוֹ לִלְמוֹד וּלְלַמֵּד לִשְׁמוֹר וְלַעֲשׂוֹת.

רַבִּי צָדוֹק אוֹמֵר: אַל תִּפְרוֹשׁ מִן הַצִּבּוּר, וְאַל תַּעַשׂ עַצְמְךָ כְעוֹרְכֵי הַדַּיָּנִין, וְאַל תַּעֲשֶׂהָ עֲטָרָה לְהִתְגַּדֵּל בָּהּ, וְלֹא קַרְדּוֹם לַחְתָּךְ בָּהּ, וְכָךְ הָיָה הִלֵּל אוֹמֵר: וּדְאִשְׁתַּמֵּשׁ בְּתַגָּא חֳלָף, הָא לָמַדְתָּ, כָּל הַנֶּהֱנֶה מִדִּבְרֵי תוֹרָה, נוֹטֵל חַיָּיו מִן הָעוֹלָם.

ו. רַבִּי יוֹסֵי אוֹמֵר: כָּל הַמְכַבֵּד אֶת הַתּוֹרָה, גּוּפוֹ מְכֻבָּד עַל הַבְּרִיּוֹת, וְכָל הַמְחַלֵּל אֶת הַתּוֹרָה, גּוּפוֹ מְחֻלָּל עַל הַבְּרִיּוֹת.

ז. רַבִּי יִשְׁמָעֵאל בְּנוֹ אוֹמֵר: הַחֹשֵׂךְ עַצְמוֹ מִן הַדִּין, פּוֹרֵק מִמֶּנּוּ אֵיבָה וְגָזֵל וּשְׁבוּעַת שָׁוְא, וְהַגַּס לִבּוֹ בְּהוֹרָאָה, שׁוֹטֶה רָשָׁע וְגַס רוּחַ.

---

thereby demonstrating that no letter is without significance.

Creatures. One must make the Torah honorable even in the eyes of "creatures"—those whose only redeeming factor is that they are G-d's creations (see above 1:12; 4:1)—by explaining the Torah to them in a way they can comprehend (*Biurim*).

His body is honored. One who seeks to protect the honor of Torah even in the face of lowly "creatures" may worry about harmful repercussions. R. Yosay therefore tells him that his body will not be harmed. On the contrary, the "creatures" will respect him for standing tall in regard to all matters of Torah and not compromising on his beliefs (*Biurim*; see also *Chelek Yaakov*).

7. One who removes himself from judgment. Instead of going to court, he works out an agreeable compromise with the other party (*Rashi*).

Most commentators read the

Mishnah as an instruction to the judge to avoid handing down a ruling and instead to work out a compromise between the litigants (*Meiri, Bartenura*).

Alternatively, the judge should remove *himself*—his ego and personal inclinations—from the ruling. Sensing his sincerity, the litigants will happily submit to his ruling (*Chelek Yaakov*).

One who acts arrogantly in...ruling. I.e., without deliberation (*Bartenura*).

A fool. The fool is eager to speak; the wise one prefers silence (*Maharal*).

● The humble person recognizes the depth of Torah and the inadequacy of the human mind. He realizes that the Torah belongs to the realm of the eternal, while he belongs to the realm of the transient. He is therefore cautious to declare that he is certain of the Torah law in a given case (*Maharal*).

studies in order to practice, is given the opportunity to study and to teach, to keep [the *mitzvot*] and to practice.

R. Tzadok said: Do not separate yourself from the community; and do not act as a counselor [when sitting as a judge]; do not make it [the Torah] a crown for self-aggrandizement, nor an axe with which to cut. So too Hillel used to say: He who exploits the crown [of Torah for his own needs] will fade away.[6] Indeed, you have learned from this: Whoever derives personal gain from the words of Torah removes his life from the world.

6. R. Yosay said: Whoever honors the Torah is (*lit.* his body is) honored by the creatures; and whoever desecrates the Torah is (*lit.* his body is) desecrated by the creatures.

7. R. Yishmael his son said: One who removes himself from judgment [and works out an agreeable compromise instead] removes from himself hatred, theft and [the responsibility for] an unnecessary oath. One who acts arrogantly in issuing a ruling is a fool, an evildoer, and a haughty spirit.

To practice. I.e., to apply his studies practically and to teach others to practice (*Midrash Shmuel*).

To keep and to practice. *To keep* from transgressing the negative commandments; *to practice*, i.e., to fulfill the positive commandments (*Midrash Shmuel*).

Do not make it a crown. The beginning of the Mishnah speaks about the positive motivations for study —to teach or to practice. This statement warns about improper motivations, such as honor and power (*Maharal*).

To cut. I.e., to earn a living. A person should not study Torah with the intention of using it as a means to earn a living (*Mefarshim*).

Exploits the crown. This refers to a person who studies Torah for self-aggrandizement or other negative reasons. Nevertheless, if this is his only motivation, he should continue to study, since the study of Torah under any condition will lead him to sincere study (*Maharal*).

From the world. I.e., from the World to Come (*Rambam*).

6. Honors the Torah. Honoring Torah encompasses many things, such as studying Torah in a respectful manner, respecting Torah books, etc. (*Mefarshim*).

Bartenura states that there is no greater way to honor Torah than by interpreting every nuance of its words,

---

6. V. supra, 1:13.

ח. הוּא הָיָה אוֹמֵר: אַל תְּהִי דָן יְחִידִי, שֶׁאֵין דָּן יְחִידִי אֶלָּא אֶחָד, וְאַל תֹּאמַר קַבְּלוּ דַעְתִּי, שֶׁהֵן רַשָּׁאִין וְלֹא אָתָּה.

ט. רַבִּי יוֹנָתָן אוֹמֵר: כָּל הַמְקַיֵּם אֶת הַתּוֹרָה מֵעֹנִי, סוֹפוֹ לְקַיְּמָהּ מֵעֹשֶׁר, וְכָל הַמְבַטֵּל אֶת הַתּוֹרָה מֵעֹשֶׁר, סוֹפוֹ לְבַטְּלָהּ מֵעֹנִי.

י. רַבִּי מֵאִיר אוֹמֵר: הֱוֵי מְמַעֵט בְּעֵסֶק וַעֲסוֹק בַּתּוֹרָה, וֶהֱוֵי שְׁפַל רוּחַ בִּפְנֵי כָל אָדָם, וְאִם בָּטַלְתָּ מִן הַתּוֹרָה, יֶשׁ לְךָ בְּטֵלִים הַרְבֵּה כְּנֶגְדֶּךָ, וְאִם עָמַלְתָּ בַּתּוֹרָה הַרְבֵּה, יֶשׁ שָׂכָר הַרְבֵּה לִתֶּן לָךְ.

יא. רַבִּי אֱלִיעֶזֶר בֶּן יַעֲקֹב אוֹמֵר: הָעוֹשֶׂה מִצְוָה אַחַת, קוֹנֶה לוֹ פְּרַקְלִיט אֶחָד, וְהָעוֹבֵר עֲבֵרָה אַחַת, קוֹנֶה לוֹ קַטֵּגוֹר אֶחָד,

---

tellectual and spiritual poverty as well. When a person fulfills Torah even amid spiritual poverty and lack of inspiration, he is promised that in the end he will fulfill it amid spiritual light and inspiration. Even as we serve G-d today in the darkness of Exile, we are promised that we will merit to serve Him in the rich light of the Messianic future (see *Midrash Shmuel* and *Knesset Yisrael*).

10. Be of humble spirit. There are two types of people: those whose primary occupation is Torah and those whose primary occupation is business. The businessman who minimizes his business affairs to study Torah creates a third group with the advantages of both. This may lead him to look down upon the other groups. The Mishnah therefore warns him: be humble before every person (*Biurim*).

● Ponder the fact that we are all like one body. Even if you are the "head," you still need the "feet" to reach your goal (see *Biurim*).

Many distractions before you. Literally, the phrase means: *you have many "idle beings" opposite you.*

When you study Torah, all the mundane activities of your life are uplifted, since they support and facilitate your study. But if you do not study, you render *all* of your activities idleness (*Yalkut Hagershuni*).

11. Do not belittle the performance of any mitzvah. Even if you have only done one mitzvah, you already have one advocate.

The same is true of sin. Do not think that the sin nullifies the mitzvah or vice versa—each produces an independent consequence.

If you have already done many negative deeds, do not give up hope: repentance and bettering your deeds are like a shield against punishment (see *Meiri*).

Acquires. One who does a mitzvah —regardless of motivation—acquires an advocating angel (*Midrash Shmuel, Biurim*).

8. He used to say: Do not judge alone, for none can judge alone except One; and do not say, "Accept my view," for they are allowed and not you.

9. R. Yonatan said: Whoever fulfills the Torah out of poverty will in the end fulfill it out of wealth; whoever neglects the Torah out of wealth will in the end neglect it out of poverty.

10. R. Meir said: Minimize your business activities and occupy yourself with Torah. Be of humble spirit before every person. If you distract yourself from Torah, you will have many distractions before you, but if you toil much in Torah, there is much reward to be given you.

11. R. Eliezer ben Yaakov said: He who does one mitzvah acquires for himself one advocate, and he who commits one transgression

---

8. Do not judge alone. Although it is legally permitted for a true expert to judge alone (see *Sanhedrin* 5a), he should go beyond the letter of the law and include other judges in the decision (*Rambam*).

● *R. Yaakov of Amshinov* offers this interpretation: When you judge a person, do not judge him *alone*, in isolation. Think of the consequences and extended ramifications of your judgment. (For example, think of the effect your judgment will have on his children and family.) Only G-d can judge the person as an individual, since He has the power to ensure that only the individual will be affected by the judgment.

None can judge alone. Only G-d is One and indivisible. Humans, by contrast, are composite beings made up of many facets. When they judge, they do not judge "alone" with complete objective clarity—they are joined by a host of tendencies, sentiments and biases that may skew their vision. Since they are incapable of judging "alone," i.e., without bias, they should not judge alone in the literal sense but rather should join with other judges (*HaChasid*).

Do not say, "Accept my view." I.e., to the other judges. Do not say, "It was only to be humble that I asked you to join me. I am an expert and could have presided alone—so accept my view" (*Bartenura, Magen Avot*).

According to *Maharal*, the judge should not say, "accept my view" to the litigants. He should explain his reasoning to them instead of demanding that they accept his ruling without question.

They are allowed. The other judges are allowed to force their view on you because they are the majority, but you are not allowed to force your view on them (*Midrash Shmuel*).

9. Out of poverty. This refers not only to financial poverty, but to in-

תְּשׁוּבָה וּמַעֲשִׂים טוֹבִים כִּתְרִיס בִּפְנֵי הַפּוּרְעָנוּת. רַבִּי יוֹחָנָן הַסַּנְדְּלָר אוֹמֵר: כָּל כְּנֵסִיָּה שֶׁהִיא לְשֵׁם שָׁמַיִם סוֹפָהּ לְהִתְקַיֵּם, וְשֶׁאֵינָהּ לְשֵׁם שָׁמַיִם אֵין סוֹפָהּ לְהִתְקַיֵּם.

יב. רַבִּי אֶלְעָזָר בֶּן שַׁמּוּעַ אוֹמֵר: יְהִי כְבוֹד תַּלְמִידְךָ חָבִיב עָלֶיךָ כְּשֶׁלָּךְ, וּכְבוֹד חֲבֵרְךָ כְּמוֹרָא רַבָּךְ, וּמוֹרָא רַבָּךְ כְּמוֹרָא שָׁמָיִם.

יג. רַבִּי יְהוּדָה אוֹמֵר: הֱוֵי זָהִיר בְּתַלְמוּד, שֶׁשִּׁגְגַת תַּלְמוּד עוֹלָה זָדוֹן. רַבִּי שִׁמְעוֹן אוֹמֵר: שְׁלֹשָׁה כְתָרִים הֵן: כֶּתֶר תּוֹרָה, וְכֶתֶר כְּהֻנָּה, וְכֶתֶר מַלְכוּת, וְכֶתֶר שֵׁם טוֹב עוֹלֶה עַל גַּבֵּיהֶן.

יד. רַבִּי נְהוֹרַאי אוֹמֵר: הֱוֵי גוֹלֶה לִמְקוֹם תּוֹרָה, וְאַל תֹּאמַר שֶׁהִיא תָבוֹא אַחֲרֶיךָ, שֶׁחֲבֵרֶיךָ יְקַיְּמוּהָ בְיָדֶךָ, וְאַל בִּינָתְךָ אַל תִּשָּׁעֵן.

---

sees the manifestation of this Mishnah in the endurance of the Jewish people: *"Look and see what G-d has done for you! It is close to two thousand years that you are exiled in a land not your own, yet your assembly has endured. How many ancient and awesome nations have disappeared from the world during this time?.... The same is true of the Sadducees, who were numerous and strong in the times of the Temple but whose name disappeared after the Exile like the morning clouds. For falsehood has no legs. But you who cleave to the living G-d... He will not abandon His nation, He will once again have mercy on us, He will renew our days as of old..."* (*Lechem Shamayim*).

12. The previous Mishnah speaks about the endurance of a sacred assembly. R. Elazar adds that an assembly can be successful when the participants treat their inferiors as equals and their equals as superiors (*R. Moshe Alashkar*). The Mishnah divides one's

relationship with others into three categories—inferiors, equals and superiors—and instructs upon the proper perspective toward each group (*Abarbanel*; see also above 1:6).

13. Wanton transgression. A person who sins unwittingly due to lack of knowledge is held accountable for the deliberate act of failing to study (*Sforno*).

Crown of a good name. I.e., a good reputation caused by one's good deeds and character (*Bartenura*). A truly good name is attained through knowledge and fulfillment of Torah (*Rambam*) and is therefore not considered a fourth crown (see *Etz Yosef* cited in *Knesset Yisrael*).

14. Exile yourself. I.e., if your native city lacks Torah scholars (*Bartenura*). In a broader sense, the Mishnah instructs a student to leave his hometown to study in "exile." He can then progress uninhibited in his studies and spiritual development (see *Lev Avot*).

acquires against himself one accuser. Repentance and good deeds are like a shield against retribution. R. Yochanan the Cobbler said: Any assembly whose purpose is for the sake of Heaven will in the end endure, but one that is not for the sake of Heaven will not in the end endure.

12. R. Elazar ben Shamua said: Let the honor of your student be as dear to you as your own, the honor of your colleague as the reverence for your teacher, and the reverence for your teacher as the reverence for Heaven.

13. R. Yehudah said: Be cautious in study, for an unwitting error in [observance due to insufficient] study is accounted as wanton transgression. R. Shimon said: There are three crowns: the crown of Torah, the crown of priesthood, and the crown of kingship; and the crown of a good name surpasses them all.

14. R. Nehora'ey said: Exile yourself to a place of Torah—and do not assume that it [the Torah] will come after you—for it is your colleagues who [through discussion and deliberation] will cause it to be clearly established with you; do not rely on your own understanding.[7]

Repentance and good deeds. A mitzvah done without the proper intention is like a diamond covered with dirt. The diamond may not shine, but it is there—completely. Similarly, a mitzvah done without proper intention does not shine—but it is there completely, albeit concealed. Its "shine" will remain concealed until the person repents and elevates himself. All of his deeds are then elevated with him and they begin to shine. Hence, *repentance and good deeds*: through repentance one's deeds become "good" and luminous (*Likkutei Torah* 82a, *Biurim*).

Assembly. An alliance of diverse individuals will inevitably suffer from discord, since each person comes with his own agenda. All that can unite them is a higher purpose—awe and love of G-d. If they are focused on this goal, they will surrender to what is proper and focus on the common good instead of their own biases (*Abarbanel*).

Not for the sake of heaven. Even if the assembly is convened for positive things (it is a כנס י״ה "*Kennes Yud-Kay*," an assembly of G-d) but the motivation of the participants is tainted by selfishness—it is not purely for the sake of heaven—it will not endure (*Midrash Shmuel*).

● ETERNAL ISRAEL. R. Yaakov Emden

---

7. Proverbs 3:5.

טו. רַבִּי יַנַּאי אוֹמֵר: אֵין בְּיָדֵינוּ לֹא מִשַּׁלְוַת הָרְשָׁעִים, וְאַף לֹא מִיִּסּוּרֵי הַצַּדִּיקִים. רַבִּי מַתְיָא בֶּן חָרָשׁ אוֹמֵר: הֱוֵי מַקְדִּים בִּשְׁלוֹם כָּל אָדָם, וֶהֱוֵי זָנָב לָאֲרָיוֹת, וְאַל תְּהִי רֹאשׁ לַשּׁוּעָלִים.

טז. רַבִּי יַעֲקֹב אוֹמֵר: הָעוֹלָם הַזֶּה דּוֹמֶה לִפְרוֹזְדוֹר בִּפְנֵי הָעוֹלָם הַבָּא, הַתְקֵן עַצְמְךָ בַּפְּרוֹזְדוֹר כְּדֵי שֶׁתִּכָּנֵס לַטְּרַקְלִין.

יז. הוּא הָיָה אוֹמֵר: יָפָה שָׁעָה אַחַת בִּתְשׁוּבָה וּמַעֲשִׂים טוֹבִים בָּעוֹלָם הַזֶּה, מִכָּל חַיֵּי הָעוֹלָם הַבָּא, וְיָפָה שָׁעָה אַחַת שֶׁל קוֹרַת רוּחַ בָּעוֹלָם הַבָּא, מִכָּל חַיֵּי הָעוֹלָם הַזֶּה.

יח. רַבִּי שִׁמְעוֹן בֶּן אֶלְעָזָר אוֹמֵר: אַל תְּרַצֶּה אֶת חֲבֵרְךָ בִּשְׁעַת כַּעֲסוֹ, וְאַל תְּנַחֲמֵהוּ בְּשָׁעָה שֶׁמֵּתוֹ מֻטָּל לְפָנָיו, וְאַל תִּשְׁאַל לוֹ בִּשְׁעַת נִדְרוֹ, וְאַל תִּשְׁתַּדֵּל לִרְאוֹתוֹ בִּשְׁעַת קַלְקָלָתוֹ.

יט. שְׁמוּאֵל הַקָּטָן אוֹמֵר: בִּנְפֹל אוֹיִבְךָ אַל תִּשְׂמָח, וּבִכָּשְׁלוֹ אַל יָגֵל לִבֶּךָ, פֶּן יִרְאֶה יְיָ וְרַע בְּעֵינָיו, וְהֵשִׁיב מֵעָלָיו אַפּוֹ.

כ. אֱלִישָׁע בֶּן אֲבוּיָה אוֹמֵר, הַלּוֹמֵד תּוֹרָה יֶלֶד לְמָה הוּא דוֹמֶה:

---

deeds that are inherently positive but which achieve the opposite of their intended purpose when performed at the wrong time. An angry person only becomes angrier when others attempt to appease him; a mourner will mourn more bitterly if one fails to acknowledge his pain; one who is taking an oath will take it more forcefully if he is questioned; and the disgraced one is further disgraced in the presence of others (*Maharal*).

19. When your enemy falls. A sincere person does not take personal pleasure when he is proven right. He is concerned with the issue in question, not in personal vindication. Thus when his opponent falls and is proven wrong, he may rejoice over the fact that the truth has been brought to light, but not over his fellow's defeat (see *Biurim*).

Even if the enemy in question is an evil person, do not rejoice. The fact that his negative deeds came to your attention indicates that you suffer from the same evil on some level. By rejoicing over his downfall, you pronounce judgment upon yourself (*Biurim*).

20. Studies Torah as a child. In addition to its literal meaning, the Mishnah can also mean that a person should study with humility, as if he were a child. One who studies as an "old man"—relying entirely on his acquired wisdom and understanding—cannot be a receptacle for the Divine Torah (*Biurim*).

15. R. Yannai said: It is not in our hands [to understand] neither the tranquility of the wicked nor the tribulations of the righteous. R. Matya ben Charash said: Be first to greet every person; be a tail to lions and do not be a head to foxes.

16. R. Yaakov said: This world is like an antechamber before the World to Come; prepare yourself in the antechamber so that you may enter the banquet hall.

17. He used to say: One hour of repentance and good deeds in this world is better than all the life of the World to Come; and one hour of bliss in the World to Come is better than all the life of this world.

18. R. Shimon ben Elazar said: Do not appease your friend in the moment of his anger; do not comfort him while his dead lies before him; do not question him about his vow at the moment he makes it; and do not seek to see him at the time of his disgrace.

19. Shmuel the Small [the humble one] said: *When your enemy falls, do not rejoice, and when he stumbles let not your heart be glad, lest G-d see and be displeased, and He will divert His wrath from him [to you].*[8]

20. Elisha ben Avuya said: He who studies Torah as a child, to what

---

15. Not in our hands. Were it in our hands, the wicked would suffer and the righteous would prosper. But it is in the hands of G-d (Rashi), whose calculations are beyond us (see *Mefarshim*).

Be first to greet. Act humbly and greet people before they greet you, unlike the arrogant who wait for others to greet them (*Maharal*). Also, when involved in a dispute, be the first to offer peace (*Pri Chaim*).

Every person. Even one who seems inferior to you (*Midrash Shmuel*).

Tail to lions. Better to be a humble follower of virtuous men than the chieftain of empty ones (Rashi).

17. In this world a person has the chance to connect with the essence of G-d by fulfilling His desire that man turn the physical world into a Divine abode. However, the soul does not perceive Divine revelation in this world. In the next world, the soul does perceive Divine revelation but does not have the opportunity to connect with the Divine essence (see *Biurim*).

18. R. Shimon offers four examples of

---

8. Ibid. 24:17-18.

לְדָיוֹ כְּתוּבָה עַל נְיָר חָדָשׁ, וְהַלּוֹמֵד תּוֹרָה זָקֵן לְמָה הוּא
דוֹמֶה: לִדְיוֹ כְּתוּבָה עַל נְיָר מָחוּק. רַבִּי יוֹסֵי בַּר יְהוּדָה אִישׁ
כְּפַר הַבַּבְלִי אוֹמֵר, הַלּוֹמֵד תּוֹרָה מִן הַקְּטַנִּים, לְמָה הוּא
דוֹמֶה: לְאוֹכֵל עֲנָבִים קֵהוֹת וְשׁוֹתֶה יַיִן מִגִּתּוֹ, וְהַלּוֹמֵד תּוֹרָה
מִן הַזְּקֵנִים, לְמָה הוּא דוֹמֶה: לְאוֹכֵל עֲנָבִים בְּשׁוּלוֹת וְשׁוֹתֶה
יַיִן יָשָׁן. רַבִּי מֵאִיר אוֹמֵר: אַל תִּסְתַּכֵּל בְּקַנְקַן, אֶלָּא בְּמַה שֶּׁיֶּשׁ
בּוֹ, יֵשׁ קַנְקַן חָדָשׁ מָלֵא יָשָׁן, וְיָשָׁן שֶׁאֲפִילוּ חָדָשׁ אֵין בּוֹ.

כא. רַבִּי אֶלְעָזָר הַקַּפָּר אוֹמֵר: הַקִּנְאָה וְהַתַּאֲוָה וְהַכָּבוֹד, מוֹצִיאִין
אֶת הָאָדָם מִן הָעוֹלָם.

כב. הוּא הָיָה אוֹמֵר: הַיִּלּוֹדִים לָמוּת, וְהַמֵּתִים לִחְיוֹת (נ״א לְהַחֲיוֹת),
וְהַחַיִּים לִדּוֹן, לֵידַע וּלְהוֹדִיעַ וּלְהִוָּדַע שֶׁהוּא אֵל, הוּא
הַיּוֹצֵר, הוּא הַבּוֹרֵא, הוּא הַמֵּבִין, הוּא הַדַּיָּן, הוּא הָעֵד, הוּא
בַּעַל דִּין, הוּא עָתִיד לָדוֹן. בָּרוּךְ הוּא, שֶׁאֵין לְפָנָיו לֹא
עַוְלָה, וְלֹא שִׁכְחָה, וְלֹא מַשּׂוֹא פָנִים, וְלֹא מִקַּח שֹׁחַד, וְדַע
שֶׁהַכֹּל לְפִי הַחֶשְׁבּוֹן. וְאַל יַבְטִיחֲךָ יִצְרְךָ שֶׁהַשְּׁאוֹל בֵּית מָנוֹס
לָךְ, שֶׁעַל כָּרְחֲךָ אַתָּה נוֹצָר, וְעַל כָּרְחֲךָ אַתָּה נוֹלָד, וְעַל

---

22. Born...die. Because they are born to mortal parents, they must die a mortal death. But those who will be revived by the Immortal One will live forever (*Maharal*).

To live again. If G-d can cause those who have never lived to live, He can certainly bring to life those who have lived before (*Sanhedrin* 91a; see *R. Bachya*).

The Fashioner. The entire world is in His hands like clay in the hands of the sculptor. For He created it all out of nothingness—and continues to create it constantly (*Tanya* 2:1)—and can therefore manipulate it at will (*Bartenura*).

According to the reckoning. Each person is judged according to his nature and capabilities (see *Rambam*).

Against your will were you born. The metaphysical soul is loath to enter the coarse body. Its natural inclination is to ascend, not descend (see *Bartenura*).

Against your will you live...die. This paradox conveys the soul's mixed emotions. On the one hand it longs to escape the spiritual exile of the body and physical life—*against your will you live*. On the other hand it recognizes that only through its sojourn in the body can it actualize G-d's desire for a Divine dwelling

can he be compared? To ink written on fresh paper [which therefore does not fade]. He who studies Torah as an old person, to what can he be compared? To ink written on worn paper [which therefore fades]. R. Yosay bar Yehudah of Kfar Habavli said: He who learns Torah from the young, to what can he be compared? To one who eats unripe grapes and drinks wine from his vat. He who learns Torah from the old, to what can he be compared? To one who eats ripe grapes and drinks aged wine. R. Meir said: Do not look at the vessel, but at its contents: there may be a new vessel filled with aged wine, or an old vessel that does not contain even new wine.

21. R. Elazar HaKappar said: Envy, lust and [pursuit of] honor drive a person from the world.

22. He used to say: Those who are born are destined to die; those who are dead are destined to live again (*another version*: to be resurrected); and those who live [again] are destined to be judged. [Therefore, let man] know, make known, and become aware that He is G-d, He is the Fashioner, He is the Creator, He is the Discerner, He is the Judge, He is the Witness, He is the Plaintiff, He will hereafter sit in judgment. Blessed is He, before whom there is neither iniquity nor forgetting, neither partiality nor bribery; and know that all is according to the reckoning. Let not your evil inclination assure you that the grave will be a refuge for you—for against your will were you fashioned, and against your will were you born; against your will you live, and against your

---

Unripe grapes. A young teacher does not have a firm grasp of Torah and his teachings are therefore unsatisfying to his students (*Bartenura*).

Wine from his vat. I.e., wine that is still mixed with sediment. Similarly, the young teacher's wisdom lacks complete clarity (*Bartenura*).

Do not look at the vessel. R. Meir argues that the age of the teacher is not always significant (*Meiri*). In a broader sense, R. Meir instructs against judging people and things based on their appearance (*R.Y. ben Shlomo*).

21. These three vices weaken a person's physical health—driving him from this world—and destroy his spiritual life, driving him from the World to Come (*HaChasid*).

כָּרְחָךָ אַתָּה חַי, וְעַל כָּרְחָךָ אַתָּה מֵת, וְעַל כָּרְחָךָ אַתָּה עָתִיד
לִתֵּן דִּין וְחֶשְׁבּוֹן לִפְנֵי מֶלֶךְ מַלְכֵי הַמְּלָכִים, הַקָּדוֹשׁ בָּרוּךְ
הוּא.

רַבִּי חֲנַנְיָא בֶּן עֲקַשְׁיָא אוֹמֵר: רָצָה הַקָּדוֹשׁ בָּרוּךְ הוּא לְזַכּוֹת אֶת יִשְׂרָאֵל,
לְפִיכָךְ הִרְבָּה לָהֶם תּוֹרָה וּמִצְוֹת, שֶׁנֶּאֱמַר: יְיָ חָפֵץ לְמַעַן צִדְקוֹ, יַגְדִּיל
תּוֹרָה וְיַאְדִּיר.

yearning for transcendence vs. pragmatic immanence—are crucial: yearning for transcendence itself is not a
worthy goal, since it is only through a
sanctified *physical* life that the Divine
mission is fulfilled. But one who becomes comfortable in the spiritual exile of physical existence, will likely
lose perspective and fail in his mission
(*Biurim*).

will you die; and against your will are you destined to give an account before the supreme King of kings, the Holy One, blessed be He.

———————

Rabbi Chananyah ben Akashya said: The Holy One, blessed be He, wished to make Israel meritorious. He therefore increased for them Torah and mitzvot, as it says: *G-d desired, for the sake of his [Israel's] righteousness, to make the Torah great and glorious.*[9] (*Makkot* 3:16)

———————

within physical reality. It identifies so strongly with this Divine will that it does not wish to part from this world—*against your will you die* (see above, Mishnah 17; *Tanyah* ch. 50).

These two conflicting drives—

———————

9. Isaiah 42:21.

פֶּרֶק חֲמִישִׁי

כָּל יִשְׂרָאֵל יֵשׁ לָהֶם חֵלֶק לְעוֹלָם הַבָּא, שֶׁנֶּאֱמַר: וְעַמֵּךְ כֻּלָּם צַדִּיקִים, לְעוֹלָם יִירְשׁוּ אָרֶץ, נֵצֶר מַטָּעַי מַעֲשֵׂה יָדַי לְהִתְפָּאֵר.

א. בַּעֲשָׂרָה מַאֲמָרוֹת נִבְרָא הָעוֹלָם, וּמַה תַּלְמוּד לוֹמַר, וַהֲלֹא בְּמַאֲמָר אֶחָד יָכוֹל לְהִבָּרְאוֹת, אֶלָּא לְהִפָּרַע מִן הָרְשָׁעִים שֶׁמְּאַבְּדִין אֶת הָעוֹלָם שֶׁנִּבְרָא בַּעֲשָׂרָה מַאֲמָרוֹת, וְלִתֵּן שָׂכָר טוֹב לַצַּדִּיקִים שֶׁמְּקַיְּמִין אֶת הָעוֹלָם שֶׁנִּבְרָא בַּעֲשָׂרָה מַאֲמָרוֹת.

ב. עֲשָׂרָה דוֹרוֹת מֵאָדָם וְעַד נֹחַ, לְהוֹדִיעַ כַּמָּה אֶרֶךְ אַפַּיִם לְפָנָיו, שֶׁכָּל הַדּוֹרוֹת הָיוּ מַכְעִיסִין וּבָאִין, עַד שֶׁהֵבִיא עֲלֵיהֶם אֶת מֵי

---

rebirths would have been less likely in this more spiritual world. G-d therefore created the world with ten utterances, a very material world of division and multiplicity, in order to create an arena for human challenge and achievement, reward and punishment (see *Midrash Shmuel* and Arizal, *Etz Chaim* 11:6).

To exact payment. G-d punishes man—not for revenge, G-d forbid, but to set him on the path of return, so that he repays what he owes and redeems himself (see *Midrash Shmuel*).

● Through repentance one surpasses the level of a *tzaddik* who has never sinned. One who experiences spiritual darkness returns to G-d with an intensity much greater than that of the *tzaddik*. He thereby elevates the negative acts he committed, since they become fuel for his return. The *tzaddik*, by contrast, serves G-d only within the realm of the permitted.

Hence: G-d creates the world with ten utterances, a world of disparity

and challenge, to "exact payment from the wicked," i.e., for the return of those who have fallen, and *secondarily*, for the straightforward service of the *tzaddikim* (see *Biurim*).

2. Adam to Noah. Adam, Seth, Enosh, Keinan, Mahalael, Yered, Enoch, Methuselah, Lemech, Noah.

Ten. Ten is the only complete unit (see above 3:6). Therefore, as long as evil had not permeated all ten aspects of the unit, there was still hope for rehabilitation. Only after ten immoral generations had passed, when evil had pervaded every aspect of the world, did G-d destroy it (see *Maharal, Biurim*).

The Flood. There are two types of evil: one that can be sublimated and one that must be destroyed. The evil of the first ten generations was such that the only way to deal with it was to destroy it. The evil of the next ten generations possessed some sparks of good, such as the fact that there was unity among the peoples. Abraham

CHAPTER FIVE

All of Israel have a share in the World to Come, as it says, *Your people are all righteous; they will inherit the Land forever; they are the branch of My planting, the work of My hands in which I take pride.*[1] (*Sanhedrin* 11:1)

1. The world was created with ten [Divine] utterances. What does this come to teach us? Surely it could have been created with one utterance! It was to exact payment from the wicked who destroy the world created by ten utterances, and to bestow ample reward upon the righteous who sustain the world created by ten utterances.

2. There were ten generations from Adam to Noah—this shows the greatness of His patience. For all those generations were repeatedly provoking, until He brought upon them the waters of the Flood.

CHAPTER FIVE. The bulk of this chapter is devoted to numbers —specifically, the numbers ten, seven and four —and, toward the end, to passages with similar constructs.

• The chapter begins with a sequential list of historical events, all of which involve the number ten: Creation, the generations from Adam to Noah and Noah to Abraham, Abraham's trials, the Exodus from Egypt and the splitting of the sea, Israel's sojourn in the desert, and finally the ten miracles in the Holy Temple in Jerusalem (see *Likkutei Sichot,* 4:1220). In each case the number ten is significant, as explained below.

1. Ten Divine utterances. The ten utterances refer to G-d's statements in the beginning of Genesis, such as "Let there be light," "Let there be a firmament," etc. The world came into being—and remains in existence—by

the power of those utterances (see *Shaar Hayichud v'haEmunah* chap. 1).

Ten. Every being is made up of ten facets. The number ten thus represents a complete unit (see above 3:6 and below). By creating the world with ten separate statements, instead of one general statement, G-d granted meaning and significance to the individual features of reality. Consequently, one's deeds—wicked or righteous—become even more significant (see *Rambam* and *Biurim*).

By giving credence to the disparate aspects of creation, G-d further concealed His being, which is epitomized by oneness, thereby increasing the challenge faced by human beings to act in a G-dly way (see below).

One utterance. A world created with one utterance would have reflected the oneness and unity of its Creator. Challenges and triumphs, failings and

---

1. Isaiah 60:21.

הַמַּבּוּל. עֲשָׂרָה דוֹרוֹת מִנֹּחַ וְעַד אַבְרָהָם, לְהוֹדִיעַ כַּמָּה אֶרֶךְ אַפַּיִם לְפָנָיו, שֶׁכָּל הַדּוֹרוֹת הָיוּ מַכְעִיסִין וּבָאִין, עַד שֶׁבָּא אַבְרָהָם אָבִינוּ וְקִבֵּל שְׂכַר כֻּלָּם.

ג. עֲשָׂרָה נִסְיוֹנוֹת נִתְנַסָּה אַבְרָהָם אָבִינוּ, וְעָמַד בְּכֻלָּם, לְהוֹדִיעַ כַּמָּה חִבָּתוֹ שֶׁל אַבְרָהָם אָבִינוּ.

ד. עֲשָׂרָה נִסִּים נַעֲשׂוּ לַאֲבוֹתֵינוּ בְמִצְרַיִם, וַעֲשָׂרָה עַל הַיָּם. עֶשֶׂר מַכּוֹת הֵבִיא הַקָּדוֹשׁ בָּרוּךְ הוּא עַל הַמִּצְרִיִּים בְּמִצְרַיִם, וְעֶשֶׂר עַל הַיָּם. עֲשָׂרָה נִסְיוֹנוֹת נִסּוּ אֲבוֹתֵינוּ אֶת הַקָּדוֹשׁ בָּרוּךְ הוּא בַּמִּדְבָּר, שֶׁנֶּאֱמַר: וַיְנַסּוּ אֹתִי זֶה עֶשֶׂר פְּעָמִים, וְלֹא שָׁמְעוּ בְּקוֹלִי.

ה. עֲשָׂרָה נִסִּים נַעֲשׂוּ לַאֲבוֹתֵינוּ בְּבֵית הַמִּקְדָּשׁ: לֹא הִפִּילָה אִשָּׁה

Ten Tests. Such as being asked by G-d to leave his native land, to circumcise himself and his son, to sacrifice Isaac, etc. (see *Rashi*).

4. Ten miracles...in Egypt. While the Egyptians suffered through the ten plagues, the neighboring Israelites were miraculously spared (*Rambam*). The Israelites were uplifted by these miracles and the process of redemption was begun (see *Biurim*).

Ten miracles at the sea. In addition to the splitting of the sea, there were many other miracles that occurred at that time, such as the fact that the ground dried and hardened for the Israelites but was wet and cement-like for the Egyptians (see *Rambam*).

● The destruction of Egypt and the Divine revelation at the sea were integral to the development of the Jewish nation.
    Both events pervaded all ten aspects of reality—every evil aspect of Egypt was negated and Divine revelation permeated every aspect of nature (see *Maharal*).

Ten plagues at the sea. The Egyptians experienced many plagues at the sea, all of which were variations on those they suffered in Egypt (*Rambam*).

Ten trials. Such as their complaint while descending toward the sea: "Are there no graves in Egypt that you took us to die in the desert?" (see *Rashi*).
    They tested G-d thoroughly—in ten different ways—and G-d proved Himself to them in every case. The Israelites were thereby uplifted and their belief strengthened (*Biurim*; see also *Maharam Shik*).

5. The common theme conveyed by these miracles is that no harm came about inside the Holy Temple—from the most severe harm: miscarriage, to the least severe: the discomfort of overcrowding (*Maharal*).

There were ten generations from Noah to Abraham—this shows the greatness of His patience. For all those generations were repeatedly provoking, until Abraham our father came and received the reward of them all.

3. With ten tests was our father Abraham tested, and he withstood them all—this shows the greatness of our father Abraham's love for G-d.

4. Ten miracles were performed for our forefathers in Egypt and ten at the Sea. Ten plagues did the Holy One, blessed be He, bring upon the Egyptians in Egypt and ten at the Sea. With ten trials did our forefathers try the Holy One, blessed be He, in the desert, as it says: *By now they have tested Me ten times and did not heed My voice.*[2]

5. Ten miracles were wrought for our forefathers in the Holy Tem-

---

was therefore able to redeem that world through his deeds (*Biurim*).

Noah to Abraham. Shem, Arpachshad, Shelach, Ever, Peleg, Reu, Serug, Nachor, Terach, Abraham.

Abraham…received the reward. The first twenty generations of humanity were unable to reconcile the physical and spiritual realms; heaven and earth were to them unbridgeable extremes. These two millennia are referred to in the Talmud as "chaos" (*Avoda Zara* 9a). Abraham began the era of "Torah" and demonstrated how the physical world can be a vessel for holiness through the fulfillment of physical *mitzvot*. Abraham channeled the extreme energies of the previous generation towards a holy end—"he received the reward for them all" (see *Maharal*).

[Obviously, the first two millennia were not a false start, G-d forbid. Rather, they served as the precursor and

precedent for our task in destroying and subjugating evil (see *Biurim*).]

3. Tests. The average person is capable of withstanding certain types of tests but not others. The fact that Abraham withstood *ten* tests—which encompassed the entire spectrum of his experience (ten being the complete unit)—proved that his righteousness was all-encompassing. His love for G-d was such that he was undaunted by any test, regardless of its nature (*Maharal*; see *Likutei Sichot* 20:73). As descendants of our father Abraham, we should expect tests as well. And as his descendants, we inherit the power to overcome them (*Biurim*).

● G-d foresees the future. He need not test Abraham, or anyone else, in order to see the outcome. The purpose of the test is to bring out and actualize the latent powers of the person (see *Maharal*).

---

2. Numbers 14:22.

מֵרִיחַ בְּשַׂר הַקֹּדֶשׁ, וְלֹא הִסְרִיחַ בְּשַׂר הַקֹּדֶשׁ מֵעוֹלָם, וְלֹא נִרְאָה
זְבוּב בְּבֵית הַמִּטְבָּחַיִם, וְלֹא אִירַע קֶרִי לְכֹהֵן גָּדוֹל בְּיוֹם
הַכִּפּוּרִים, וְלֹא כִבּוּ הַגְּשָׁמִים אֵשׁ שֶׁל עֲצֵי הַמַּעֲרָכָה, וְלֹא נִצְּחָה
הָרוּחַ אֶת עַמּוּד הֶעָשָׁן, וְלֹא נִמְצָא פְסוּל בָּעֹמֶר וּבִשְׁתֵּי הַלֶּחֶם
וּבְלֶחֶם הַפָּנִים, עוֹמְדִים צְפוּפִים וּמִשְׁתַּחֲוִים רְוָחִים, וְלֹא הִזִּיק
נָחָשׁ וְעַקְרָב בִּירוּשָׁלַיִם, וְלֹא אָמַר אָדָם לַחֲבֵרוֹ: צַר לִי הַמָּקוֹם
שֶׁאָלִין בִּירוּשָׁלָיִם.

ו. עֲשָׂרָה דְבָרִים נִבְרְאוּ בְּעֶרֶב שַׁבָּת בֵּין הַשְּׁמָשׁוֹת, וְאֵלּוּ הֵן: פִּי
הָאָרֶץ, פִּי הַבְּאֵר, פִּי הָאָתוֹן, הַקֶּשֶׁת, וְהַמָּן, וְהַמַּטֶּה, וְהַשָּׁמִיר,
הַכְּתָב, וְהַמִּכְתָּב, וְהַלֻּחוֹת. וְיֵשׁ אוֹמְרִים: אַף קִבְרוֹ שֶׁל מֹשֶׁה

---

altar. If the loaves were disqualified, others could not be baked (because doing so would desecrate the festival) and the opportunity would be lost (*Mefarshim*).

Showbread. The showbread was prepared on Friday and placed on the Table in the Temple on Shabbat, where it remained until the next Shabbat. If the showbread was disqualified, the Table would have to remain empty all week long (*Mefarshim*).

6. Twilight. The twilight period is a time when the day has not yet ended, yet the night—which in Jewish law is the next day—has already begun.

The twilight period of the first Friday of creation contained within it elements of both Friday—a day of creation and nature—and Shabbat, a day of rest and transcendence from nature. Therefore, G-d *created* things during that time—because it was still Friday, a day of creation—but those creations were of a transcendent, miraculous sort, because it was in a sense

already Shabbat. Hence the objects described in our Mishnah—all of which, are supernatural phenomena (*Maharal*).

● All the tools necessary for man to fulfill his mission in this world were created prior to his creation. The supernatural objects mentioned in this Mishnah were created after man, since man's primary field of achievement is in the natural realm (see *Biurim*).

● Adam's sin brought to the world spiritual darkness (including the existence of destructive spirits —*Abarbanel*) that would last for generations. G-d therefore created miraculous phenomena during the twilight period after the sin to counter that darkness (see *Midrash Shmuel*).

Shamir worm. Without this worm, it would have been impossible to cut the stones for the Temple, since the Torah prohibits the use of metal—because of its association with weaponry—in the construction of the Temple (see *Gittin* 68a).

ple: No woman miscarried because of the aroma of the meat of the holy sacrifices; the meat of the holy sacrifices never became putrid; no fly was seen in the slaughter-house; no bodily impurity befell the High Priest on Yom Kippur; the rains did not extinguish the fire on the wood-pile on the altar; the wind did not prevail over the column of smoke [arising from the altar-fire]; no disqualifying defect was found in the *omer*,[3] or in the Two [Shavuot] Loaves,[4] or in the Showbread[5]; the worshippers stood crammed together, yet prostrated with ample space; no serpent or scorpion caused harm in Jerusalem; no man said to his fellow, "The space is too crowded for me to lodge overnight in Jerusalem."

6. Ten things were created on the eve of Shabbat at twilight [on the sixth day of creation]. They are: The mouth of the earth [to swallow Korach][6]; the mouth of the well [that gave water to the Israelites in the desert][7]; the mouth of [Balaam's talking] donkey[8]; the rainbow[9] [that appeared after the Flood]; the manna[10]; the staff [of Moshe][11]; the *shamir* worm [that split stones for the Holy Temple][12]; the form of the letters [of the Tablets][13]; the engraving [of the Tablets][14]; and the Tablets.[15] Some add the burial place of Moshe[16] and the ram of Abraham our father.[17] And

---

Aroma of meat. If a pregnant woman smells food and craves it, her life and the life of her fetus are in danger until she partakes of it (see *Yoma* 82a). Miraculously, the aroma of the meat roasting in the Temple never tempted pregnant women. The purpose of this miracle was to ensure that pregnant women would feel comfortable coming to the Temple (*Tiferet Yisrael*).

The *omer*. The *omer* was a barley offering that was brought on the second day of Passover from barley harvested the night before. If a defect was found in the *omer*, it could not be replaced, since the exact amount of barley was harvested the night before for this purpose. If the *omer* was not offered on that day, it could not be offered at all (*Mefarshim*; see *Menachot* 68b).

Loaves. Two loaves made of wheat were prepared on the eve of Shavuot and offered on Shavuot. Once these were offered, the grain of the new crop became permitted for use on the

---

3. V. Leviticus 23:9-14.   4. V. Ibid. 23:16-17.   5. V. Exodus 25:30; Leviticus 24:5-8.   6. Numbers 16:32.   7. Ibid. 21:16-18; Exodus 17:6.   8. Numbers 22:28.   9. Genesis 9:13.   10. Exodus 16:11-15; 31-36.   11. Ibid. 4:17.   12. V. Gittin 68a; Sotah 48b.   13. Exodus 34:1.   14. Ibid. 32:16.   15. Loc. cit.   16. V. Deuteronomy 34:6.   17. V. Genesis 22:13.

רַבֵּנוּ, וְאִילוּ שֶׁל אַבְרָהָם אָבִינוּ. וְיֵשׁ אוֹמְרִים: אַף הַמַּזִּיקִין, וְאַף צְבַת בִּצְבַת עֲשׂוּיָה.

ז. שִׁבְעָה דְבָרִים בַּגּוֹלֶם וְשִׁבְעָה בֶּחָכָם, חָכָם: אֵינוֹ מְדַבֵּר לִפְנֵי מִי שֶׁגָּדוֹל מִמֶּנּוּ בְּחָכְמָה וּבְמִנְיָן, וְאֵינוֹ נִכְנָס לְתוֹךְ דִּבְרֵי חֲבֵרוֹ, וְאֵינוֹ נִבְהָל לְהָשִׁיב, שׁוֹאֵל כָּעִנְיָן וּמֵשִׁיב כַּהֲלָכָה, וְאוֹמֵר עַל רִאשׁוֹן רִאשׁוֹן וְעַל אַחֲרוֹן אַחֲרוֹן, וְעַל מַה שֶּׁלֹּא שָׁמַע אוֹמֵר לֹא שָׁמָעְתִּי, וּמוֹדֶה עַל הָאֱמֶת, וְחִלּוּפֵיהֶן בַּגּוֹלֶם.

ח. שִׁבְעָה מִינֵי פוּרְעָנִיּוֹת בָּאִין לְעוֹלָם, עַל שִׁבְעָה גוּפֵי עֲבֵרָה: מִקְצָתָן מְעַשְּׂרִין וּמִקְצָתָן אֵינָן מְעַשְּׂרִין, רָעָב שֶׁל מְהוּמָה בָּא, מִקְצָתָן רְעֵבִים וּמִקְצָתָן שְׂבֵעִים. גָּמְרוּ שֶׁלֹּא לְעַשֵּׂר, רָעָב שֶׁל בַּצֹּרֶת בָּא. וְשֶׁלֹּא לִטּוֹל אֶת הַחַלָּה, רָעָב שֶׁל כְּלָיָה בָּא. דֶּבֶר בָּא

---

ized by seven traits, each of which reflects a structured and ordered mindset (*Maharal*).

8. Seven. As mentioned, seven represents order. When the *mitzvot* are performed properly, the order of the world is maintained. Neglect of *mitzvot* creates disorder (*Maharal*).

(Although fourteen sins are enumerated between this Mishnah and the next, they are referred to as seven, since there are seven types of sins. Those that cause the same punishment are considered to be of one type (*Maharal*).)

Punishment comes. When people withhold the sustenance of others, the sustenance of the world is correspondingly withheld (see *Maharal* and *Meiri*).

Divine punishment is not arbitrary. G-d structured the world in such a way that a misdeed results in negative repercussions that mirror the misdeed. A person can then identify his error, since it is reflected in the nature of his misfortune (see *Mefarshim*).

Famine. If only some fail to tithe, a famine caused by **upheaval** ensues. The upheaval makes tending to the fields difficult and food becomes scarce. If all decide not to tithe, a famine of drought ensues and all go hungry but some sustenance remains. If they additionally decide not to separate *challah*, a **famine of destruction** ensues—no food is available at all (see *Mefarshim*).

Challah. According to Torah law, a small portion of dough must be set aside for the *kohen* from certain dough mixtures (see Numbers 15:20). This portion is called *challah*.

Death penalties. Certain sins carry the death penalty but are not punishable by a human court. When such sins become rampant, deathly plagues afflict the world (*Rashi*).

others add the spirits of destruction,[18] as well as [tongs, since] tongs are made with tongs.

7.   There are seven traits possessed by the unrefined and seven by the wise. A wise person does not speak before one who is greater than he in wisdom or in years; he does not interrupt the words of his fellow; he does not rush to answer; he asks what is relevant to the subject matter and replies to the point; he speaks of first things first and of last things last; concerning that which he has not heard he says, "I have not heard"; and he acknowledges the truth. The opposite of these are possessed by the unrefined.

8.   Seven kinds of punishment come to the world for seven [kinds of] major transgressions: If some tithe and some do not, a famine caused by upheaval ensues—some go hungry and some are satiated. If all decided not to tithe, a famine of drought ensues; and if they [also] decided not to separate *challah,*[19] a famine of destruction ensues. Deadly plagues come to the world for the death

---

Tongs. The smith uses tongs to hold hot metal and form it into tools and vessels. Hence, "tongs are made with tongs," since one would need a pair of tongs to hold hot metal and form it into tongs. Who, then, created the first pair? G-d Himself (see *Pesachim* 54a).

● The original tongs represent an article that seems to have no independent purpose and serves only as an accessory for the creation of another article. In the human experience, the "original tongs" are those actions that serve only as facilitators to a meaningful act. By creating those tongs Himself, G-d grants meaning even to the accessories of life.

Only when a person transcends his inherent limitations and preconceived notions can he treat the accessories as

purposeful in their own right. When a person is animated solely by the Divine will, his performance of the mitzvah transcends the particulars of the *mitzvot*—he does not distinguish between the accessory and the mitzvah itself, since both are equally the Divine will (see above 2:1 and 4:2).

This supernatural, transcendent ability is not granted during the first six days of creation. It is a power granted by G-d at a time that draws its energy from the supernatural Shabbat (*Biurim*).

7. Seven. Seven represents order and structure. Every object has six sides and a center. The center is the point of connection that links all sides and brings order to the object.

Thus, a wise person is character-

---

18. V. Bereshit Rabbah 7:5; Tanchumah, ed. Buber, Bereshit Section 17; Yalkut, Bereshit, Section 12. 19. V. Numbers 15:20; Ezekiel 44:30.

לְעוֹלָם עַל מִיתוֹת הָאֲמוּרוֹת בַּתּוֹרָה שֶׁלֹּא נִמְסְרוּ לְבֵית דִּין,
וְעַל פֵּרוֹת שְׁבִיעִית. חֶרֶב בָּאָה לְעוֹלָם, עַל עִנּוּי הַדִּין, וְעַל עִוּוּת
הַדִּין, וְעַל הַמּוֹרִים בַּתּוֹרָה שֶׁלֹּא כַהֲלָכָה.

ט. חַיָּה רָעָה בָּאָה לְעוֹלָם עַל שְׁבוּעַת שָׁוְא וְעַל חִלּוּל הַשֵּׁם. גָּלוּת
בָּא לְעוֹלָם עַל עֲבוֹדָה זָרָה, וְעַל גִּלּוּי עֲרָיוֹת, וְעַל שְׁפִיכוּת
דָּמִים, וְעַל שְׁמִטַּת הָאָרֶץ.

בְּאַרְבָּעָה פְרָקִים הַדֶּבֶר מִתְרַבֶּה, בָּרְבִיעִית, וּבַשְּׁבִיעִית, וּבְמוֹצָאֵי
שְׁבִיעִית, וּבְמוֹצָאֵי הֶחָג שֶׁבְּכָל שָׁנָה וְשָׁנָה. בָּרְבִיעִית, מִפְּנֵי
מַעְשַׂר עָנִי שֶׁבַּשְּׁלִישִׁית. בַּשְּׁבִיעִית, מִפְּנֵי מַעְשַׂר עָנִי שֶׁבַּשִּׁשִּׁית.
בְּמוֹצָאֵי שְׁבִיעִית, מִפְּנֵי פֵּרוֹת שְׁבִיעִית. בְּמוֹצָאֵי הֶחָג שֶׁבְּכָל שָׁנָה
וְשָׁנָה, מִפְּנֵי גֶזֶל מַתְּנוֹת עֲנִיִּים.

---

of G-d—removes from himself the image of G-d, which would otherwise protect him from wild beasts (*Midrash Shmuel*; see also *Meiri*).

Exile. The Jewish people are expelled from the Land of Israel when they engage in impure activities that are incongruent with the purity of the land—such as idolatry, immorality and murder—or when they fail to keep the laws that relate to the land itself, such as the laws of the Sabbatical year (*Maharal*).

Idolatry. Each of the sins enumerated in this Mishnah can be understood on a more subtle level as well. For example, anger and arrogance are symptoms of self-worship and thus a form of "idolatry" (see *Midrash David*).

Similar abstractions can be applied to the others sins as well (see *Biurim*).

Plagues increase. Those who deprive the poor of life are deprived of their own lives (*Meiri*). Failure to give to the poor causes an *increase* in the natural level of deaths, not the more severe "plagues come to the world" mentioned in the previous Mishnah. This is because the punishment for depriving the poor is [relatively] immediate and the collective guilt never accumulates to the point that would warrant a full-scale plague coming to the world (*Maharal*).

Tithes for the poor. In addition to the regular gifts for the poor, tithes were required during the third and sixth years of the Sabbatical cycle. During the other years, tithes (or their monetary equivalent) were taken and brought to Jerusalem and consumed there by their owners.

Harvest gifts. During the harvest, the field owner must leave certain items for the poor, such as: individual fallen stalks; forgotten sheaves; and a corner of each field.

penalties enumerated in the Torah that the court was not em-
powered to carry out; and for [unlawfully making use of] the
fruits of the Sabbatical year.[20] The sword [of war] comes to the
world for [unnecessary] delay in pronouncing judgment, for the
perversion of justice and for rendering an opinion on Torah law
in a way that defies *halachah*.

9. Wild beasts come upon the world for vain oaths and for desecration of the Divine Name. Exile comes to the world for idolatry,
for sexual immorality, for murder, and for not leaving the earth
at rest during the Sabbatical year.

At four periods [of the seven-year Sabbatical cycle] deathly
plagues increase—in the fourth year, in the seventh year, in the
year following the Sabbatical year, and annually at the conclusion
of the festival of Sukkot. In the fourth year—for failure to give
the tithe for the poor in the third year; in the seventh year—for
failure to give the tithe for the poor in the sixth year; in the year
following the Sabbatical year—for [failure to observe the laws
pertaining to] the produce of the Sabbatical year; annually, at the
conclusion of the festival of Sukkot—for robbing the poor of
their [harvest] gifts.[21]

Fruits of the Sabbatical year. Every
seventh year, fields are to be treated as
ownerless. When people do not dis-
own the produce of the Sabbatical
year, the people are "disowned" and
left to the hands of the Angel of
Death (*Tiferet Yisrael*).

Unnecessary Delay. The judges see
where the case is heading and yet refrain from handing down a ruling.
This delay in judgment is torturous
for the defendant whose future remains uncertain (*Bartenura*). The
phrase also implies delaying the execution of justice, which is also tor-

turous for the condemned (*Magen
Avot*).

Defies *halachah*. I.e., forbidding the
permitted and permitting the for-
bidden (*Bartenura*).
    Failure to properly and decisively
"execute" the law results in un-
controlled "execution" by the sword
(see *Maharal*).

9. Desecration of the Divine Name.
E.g., one who sins shamelessly and
blatantly (*Bartenura*). Such a person—and the person who swears
falsely or unnecessarily by the Name

---

20. V. Exodus 23:11; Leviticus 25:1-7.   21. V. Leviticus 19:9-10; 23:22. Deuteronomy 24:19-22.

י. אַרְבַּע מִדּוֹת בָּאָדָם: הָאוֹמֵר שֶׁלִּי שֶׁלָּךְ וְשֶׁלְּךָ שֶׁלִּי, עַם הָאָרֶץ. שֶׁלִּי שֶׁלִּי וְשֶׁלְּךָ שֶׁלָּךְ, זוֹ מִדָּה בֵּינוֹנִית, וְיֵשׁ אוֹמְרִים זוֹ מִדַּת סְדוֹם. שֶׁלִּי שֶׁלָּךְ וְשֶׁלְּךָ שֶׁלָּךְ, חָסִיד. שֶׁלָּךְ שֶׁלִּי וְשֶׁלִּי שֶׁלִּי, רָשָׁע.

יא. אַרְבַּע מִדּוֹת בְּדֵעוֹת: נוֹחַ לִכְעוֹס וְנוֹחַ לִרְצוֹת, יָצָא הֶפְסֵדוֹ בִּשְׂכָרוֹ. קָשֶׁה לִכְעוֹס וְקָשֶׁה לִרְצוֹת, יָצָא שְׂכָרוֹ בְּהֶפְסֵדוֹ. קָשֶׁה לִכְעוֹס וְנוֹחַ לִרְצוֹת, חָסִיד. נוֹחַ לִכְעוֹס וְקָשֶׁה לִרְצוֹת, רָשָׁע.

יב. אַרְבַּע מִדּוֹת בְּתַלְמִידִים: מַהֵר לִשְׁמוֹעַ וּמַהֵר לְאַבֵּד, יָצָא שְׂכָרוֹ בְּהֶפְסֵדוֹ. קָשֶׁה לִשְׁמוֹעַ וְקָשֶׁה לְאַבֵּד, יָצָא הֶפְסֵדוֹ בִּשְׂכָרוֹ. מַהֵר לִשְׁמוֹעַ וְקָשֶׁה לְאַבֵּד, זֶה חֵלֶק טוֹב. קָשֶׁה לִשְׁמוֹעַ וּמַהֵר לְאַבֵּד, זֶה חֵלֶק רָע.

---

are slow to anger, but once angered are not easily appeased.

One who is slow to anger—i.e., a deliberate person—yet forgives quickly (an impetuous act), is obviously defying his nature and is therefore called pious. One who is easily angered—i.e., an impetuous person—yet does not forgive easily, is clearly a wicked person since he defies his nature to act wickedly (*Maharal*).

● Alternatively, the Mishnah refers to one whose *nature* is to get angry but who overcomes his temperament and acts properly. Still he is called "wicked," by the standards of Avot, since he must strive to change his nature (*Biurim*; see *Maharam Shik*).

12. Quick to grasp and quick to forget. This student is encouraged to review his studies and not to be satis-

fied with his quick grasp of the subject matter (*Biurim*).

Slow to grasp and slow to forget. The Mishnah encourages this student, who may feel disheartened, by saying that his advantage outweighs his disadvantage (*Biurim*).

Good portion. By recognizing that his success is due to his "good portion" granted to him by G-d, this student will not become arrogant (*Biurim*).

Bad portion. Although he has a bad portion, it is the one given to him by G-d so that he can transform it through effort to a good portion (*Biurim*). His reward will then be greater than that of one blessed with a good portion from the start (*Be'er Avot* in *Likkutei Battar Likkutei*).

10. There are four types among people: One who says, "Mine is yours, and yours is mine" is an ignoramus. "Mine is mine, and yours is yours"—this is the average characteristic; and some say this is the characteristic of Sodom. "Mine is yours, and yours is yours"—is a *chasid* (pious, benevolent person). "Yours is mine, and mine is mine"—is a wicked person.

11. There are four types among temperaments: Easily angered and easily appeased—his gain outweighs his loss; slow to anger and slow to be appeased—his loss outweighs his gain; slow to anger and easily appeased—a *chasid*; easily angered and slow to be appeased—a wicked person.

12. There are four types among students: Quick to grasp and quick to forget—his loss outweighs his gain; slow to grasp and slow to forget—his gain outweighs his loss; quick to grasp and slow to forget—this is a good portion; slow to grasp and quick to forget—this is a bad portion.

---

10. Mine is yours and yours is mine. Although this communalist attitude seems to increase brotherhood and love, its protagonist is an ignoramus, since a wise person despises taking from others (*R. Yonah, Maharal*). [He is also ignorant of the need for individual achievement and ambition, which is obscured in the communalist society (see *Be'er Avot* in *Likkutei Battar Likkutei; Igrot Kodesh* 23:263).]

Mine is mine and yours is yours... average...Sodom. According to R. Yonah, this person actually does give to others. Despite his selfishness, he forces himself to give; he only *says* "Mine is mine." The first opinion focuses on his action— which is average; the second, on his nature—Sodom-like.

Yours is mine and mine is mine. In addition to its literal meaning, the phrase can be explained as follows: In *practice*, this individual may be an openhanded benefactor. But if he is condescending toward his beneficiary, if he *says* to him—verbally or otherwise—"yours is mine," he is considered wicked (*Biurim*; see Laban's comment to Jacob, Gen. 31:43).

11. Easily angered and easily appeased. Such a person is less stressful to those around him since they know that his anger will soon pass. Not so in the case of one who is slow to anger and slow to be appeased. His anger may not flare often, but it is much more destructive when it does surface (*R. Matityahu Hayitzhari*).

● Some people are impetuous—easily angered and easily pacified. Some people act more deliberately—they

יג. אַרְבַּע מִדּוֹת בְּנוֹתְנֵי צְדָקָה: הָרוֹצֶה שֶׁיִּתֵּן וְלֹא יִתְּנוּ אֲחֵרִים, עֵינוֹ
רָעָה בְּשֶׁל אֲחֵרִים. יִתְּנוּ אֲחֵרִים וְהוּא לֹא יִתֵּן, עֵינוֹ רָעָה בְּשֶׁלּוֹ.
יִתֵּן וְיִתְּנוּ אֲחֵרִים, חָסִיד. לֹא יִתֵּן וְלֹא יִתְּנוּ אֲחֵרִים, רָשָׁע.

יד. אַרְבַּע מִדּוֹת בְּהוֹלְכֵי בֵית הַמִּדְרָשׁ: הוֹלֵךְ וְאֵינוֹ עוֹשֶׂה, שְׂכַר
הֲלִיכָה בְּיָדוֹ. עוֹשֶׂה וְאֵינוֹ הוֹלֵךְ, שְׂכַר מַעֲשֶׂה בְּיָדוֹ. הוֹלֵךְ
וְעוֹשֶׂה, חָסִיד. לֹא הוֹלֵךְ וְלֹא עוֹשֶׂה, רָשָׁע.

טו. אַרְבַּע מִדּוֹת בְּיוֹשְׁבִים לִפְנֵי חֲכָמִים: סְפוֹג, וּמַשְׁפֵּךְ, מְשַׁמֶּרֶת,
וְנָפָה. סְפוֹג, שֶׁהוּא סוֹפֵג אֶת הַכֹּל. וּמַשְׁפֵּךְ, שֶׁמַּכְנִיס בְּזוֹ וּמוֹצִיא
בְזוֹ. מְשַׁמֶּרֶת, שֶׁמּוֹצִיאָה אֶת הַיַּיִן וְקוֹלֶטֶת אֶת הַשְּׁמָרִים. וְנָפָה,
שֶׁמּוֹצִיאָה אֶת הַקֶּמַח וְקוֹלֶטֶת אֶת הַסֹּלֶת:

---

not put effort into studying Torah and is therefore called wicked (*Meiri*).

15. In addition to its literal meaning, the Mishnah can refer to various stages experienced by each student:

Sponge: When a child begins studying, he is like a sponge that absorbs everything indiscriminately—the essential and nonessential (see *Bartenura*). The teacher must bear this in mind and recognize the enormity of his responsibility (see *Biurim*).

Funnel: When the child grows tired, he becomes like a funnel and can no longer retain the teacher's words. The teacher must then grant the child a break.

Strainer: As the student grows older, he gains the capacity to discriminate between teachings. However, he is not yet capable of grasping abstract, spiritual concepts. He therefore retains the "sediment"—the hard, concrete language in which these abstractions are couched, while the refined "wine," the essence of the concept, flows past him. He must strive to reach the level of the *sieve*, which eliminates the unessential flour-dust and retains the fine flour (*Biurim*).

Funnel. The Mishnah informs the forgetful student that he too is among those who sit before the sages and that with study and review he will succeed (*Biurim*).

Alternatively, this student is a selfless conduit, who conveys the teachings of his master to others (see *Midrash Shmuel; Biurim*).

Strainer. He forgets everything he has learned in the study hall and retains only some idle thought (*Bartenura*).

Alternatively, the "strainer" student passes on the "fine wine" of his master's teachings, while retaining those sensitive aspects that would only be "sediment" in the hands of their recipients (see *Midrash Shmuel; Biurim*).

13. There are four types among charity givers: One who wishes to give but that others should not—he is resentful of others; that others should give and he should not—he is resentful of [giving away] his own; that he should give and others should give as well is a *chasid*; that neither he nor others should give is a wicked person.

14. There are four types among those who go to the House of Study: One who goes but does not succeed [in study] earns the reward for going; one who succeeds but does not go earns the reward for the act [of studying]; one who goes and succeeds is a *chasid*; one who neither goes nor succeeds is a wicked person.

15. There are four types among those who sit before the sages: a sponge, a funnel, a strainer, and a sieve. A sponge, which absorbs everything; a funnel, which takes in from one end and spills out from the other; a strainer, which allows the wine to flow through and retains the sediment; and a sieve, which allows the flour-dust to pass through and retains the fine flour.

13-14. THE CHARITABLE MISER. Although some of the characters in both 13 and 14 neither give charity nor attend the study hall, the Mishnah still refers to them as charity givers and study hall attendees. For the true desire of every person is to fulfill G-d's will. Thus even the miser should be viewed as a charity-giver and even the one who never attends should be seen as a study hall attendee because of his dormant desire. When he is viewed in this way, his dormant desire is more likely to become manifest (*Biurim*).

13. He should give and others should give. Not only does he not resent the generosity of others, he actively encourages them to give (*Maharal*).

Wicked. In addition to its plain meaning, the phrase can be rendered as follows: This individual may give charity in actuality but he does not *wish* to give it and wishes others would not give either. He would prefer that the poor slave for their sustenance. For this preference he is called wicked (*Midrash Shmuel*).

14. The reward for going. Although he does not succeed in his study or in changing his character based on the moral teachings he hears, he receives reward for going to a place of Torah (*Meiri, Tiferet Yisrael*).

One who succeeds but does not go. He studies at home and succeeds. Although he would enjoy greater success if he would go to a place of Torah, he is rewarded for his study (*Meiri*).

Neither succeeds nor goes. He does

טז. כָּל אַהֲבָה שֶׁהִיא תְלוּיָה בְדָבָר, בָּטֵל דָּבָר בְּטֵלָה אַהֲבָה, וְשֶׁאֵינָהּ תְלוּיָה בְדָבָר, אֵינָהּ בְּטֵלָה לְעוֹלָם. אֵיזוֹ הִיא אַהֲבָה שֶׁהִיא תְלוּיָה בְדָבָר, זוֹ אַהֲבַת אַמְנוֹן וְתָמָר, וְשֶׁאֵינָהּ תְלוּיָה בְדָבָר, זוֹ אַהֲבַת דָּוִד וִיהוֹנָתָן.

יז. כָּל מַחֲלוֹקֶת שֶׁהִיא לְשֵׁם שָׁמַיִם, סוֹפָהּ לְהִתְקַיֵּם, וְשֶׁאֵינָהּ לְשֵׁם שָׁמַיִם, אֵין סוֹפָהּ לְהִתְקַיֵּם. אֵיזוֹ הִיא מַחֲלוֹקֶת שֶׁהִיא לְשֵׁם שָׁמַיִם, זוֹ מַחֲלוֹקֶת הִלֵּל וְשַׁמַּאי. וְשֶׁאֵינָהּ לְשֵׁם שָׁמַיִם, זוֹ מַחֲלוֹקֶת קֹרַח וְכָל עֲדָתוֹ.

יח. כָּל הַמְזַכֶּה אֶת הָרַבִּים, אֵין חֵטְא בָּא עַל יָדוֹ, וְכָל הַמַּחֲטִיא אֶת

---

fered in regard to certain aspects of Jewish law.

Since their views were borne of their sincere desire to interpret Torah—indeed both views reflect independent spiritual truths—their controversy endures and is studied throughout the generations (*Midrash Shmuel*; *Maharal*; *Lechem Yehudah*).

● Although in practice Jewish law follows Hillel's view, Shammai's view "will endure" in the Messianic era when Jewish law will follow Shammai (Arizal cited in *Likkutei Torah*, 1:54b; *Chida*).

Furthermore, both views will be valid simultaneously in a later, more miraculous period of the Messianic era. At that time, man will be elevated to such a degree that he will perform *mitzvot* not because they are commanded to him but because he will instinctively intuit the Divine will. He will experience the *mitzvot* in their infinite form, free of the filter now applied to them to accommodate human finiteness. *Mitzvot* will then reflect their infinite source, where op-

posites can coexist (*Biurim*; see above 2:1).

Korach. Korach and his group argued against Moshe and Aharon for selfish reasons and their rebellion did not endure: some of them went up in flames and others descended into the earth (see Numbers 16:2). The Mishnah does not say "the controversy between Korach *and Moshe*," since Moshe's side of the argument was for the sake of heaven (and the Mishnah is now giving an example of an argument that is *not* for the sake of Heaven) (*Midrash Shmuel*).

18. This Mishnah describes the power of the community—the whole is greater than the sum of its parts—and its effect on the individuals who influence it. Those who influence it positively are uplifted by its power. Those who influence it negatively are held down (see *Maharal*).

No sin shall come through him. "He should not be in Purgatory while his students are in Paradise" (*Yoma* 87a cited by *Bartenura*).

16. Any love that is dependent upon a condition—when the condition ceases, the love ceases; but if it is not dependent upon anything—it will never cease. Which is a love that is dependent upon a condition? The love of Amnon and Tamar.[22] And one that is not dependent upon anything? The love of David and Jonathan.[23]

17. Any controversy that is for the sake of Heaven is destined to endure; and that which is not for the sake of Heaven is not destined to endure. Which is a controversy that is for the sake of Heaven? The controversy between Hillel and Shammai.[24] And which is not for the sake of Heaven? The controversy of Korach and his entire group.[25]

18. Anyone who causes the masses to gain merit, no sin shall come

---

● This Mishnah and the next discuss two opposite emotions: love and dissent. In both cases the essential factor is the foundation. Love that is not based on selflessness will not endure, while dissent that is based on selflessness will produce positive and enduring results (*Midrash Shmuel*).

16. Amnon and Tamar. Amnon and Tamar were half-siblings. But Amnon's unconditional, familial love for Tamar was obscured by his love for her beauty, resulting in a conditional love. When the condition for his love ceased, his love ceased, and his unconditional, familial love remained dormant as well (*Biurim*).

The Mishnah is a metaphor for love for G-d (*Midrash Shmuel*):

Every person possesses an unconditional love for G-d. However, in the early stages of his spiritual practice, this love lies dormant. It manifests itself in conditional, self-oriented love (i.e., loving G-d for what G-d does for him).

One might assume that eliminating the conditional love will cause the unconditional love to naturally. But, as the case of Amnon demonstrates, the disappearance of the conditional love does not by default restore the unconditional love.

Man must therefore retain his conditional love until he is able to reveal his unconditional love for G-d (*Biurim*).

David and Jonathan. Although their love was initially conditional upon external factors, it matured into an unconditional love.

Similarly, a person who manifestly experiences his unconditional love for G-d—even if he has reached that state through conditional love—his love will not cease (*Biurim*).

17. Hillel and Shammai. These were two sages of the Mishnah who dif-

---

22. II Samuel 13:1 ff. 23. V. I Samuel 18:1; 20:17; II Samuel 1:26. 24. Eruvin 13b. 25. Numbers Ch. 16.

הָרַבִּים, אֵין מַסְפִּיקִין בְּיָדוֹ לַעֲשׂוֹת תְּשׁוּבָה. מֹשֶׁה זָכָה וְזִכָּה אֶת הָרַבִּים, זְכוּת הָרַבִּים תָּלוּי בּוֹ, שֶׁנֶּאֱמַר: צִדְקַת יְיָ עָשָׂה, וּמִשְׁפָּטָיו עִם יִשְׂרָאֵל. יָרָבְעָם בֶּן נְבָט חָטָא וְהֶחֱטִיא אֶת הָרַבִּים, חֵטְא הָרַבִּים תָּלוּי בּוֹ, שֶׁנֶּאֱמַר: עַל חַטֹּאות יָרָבְעָם אֲשֶׁר חָטָא, וַאֲשֶׁר הֶחֱטִיא אֶת יִשְׂרָאֵל.

יט. כָּל מִי שֶׁיֵּשׁ בּוֹ שְׁלֹשָׁה דְבָרִים הַלָּלוּ, הוּא מִתַּלְמִידָיו שֶׁל אַבְרָהָם אָבִינוּ, וּשְׁלֹשָׁה דְבָרִים אֲחֵרִים, הוּא מִתַּלְמִידָיו שֶׁל בִּלְעָם הָרָשָׁע. תַּלְמִידָיו שֶׁל אַבְרָהָם אָבִינוּ: עַיִן טוֹבָה, וְרוּחַ נְמוּכָה, וְנֶפֶשׁ שְׁפָלָה. תַּלְמִידָיו שֶׁל בִּלְעָם הָרָשָׁע: עַיִן רָעָה, וְרוּחַ גְּבוֹהָה, וְנֶפֶשׁ רְחָבָה.

מַה בֵּין תַּלְמִידָיו שֶׁל אַבְרָהָם אָבִינוּ לְתַלְמִידָיו שֶׁל בִּלְעָם הָרָשָׁע, תַּלְמִידָיו שֶׁל אַבְרָהָם אָבִינוּ אוֹכְלִין בָּעוֹלָם הַזֶּה, וְנוֹחֲלִין הָעוֹלָם הַבָּא, שֶׁנֶּאֱמַר: לְהַנְחִיל אֹהֲבַי יֵשׁ, וְאוֹצְרֹתֵיהֶם אֲמַלֵּא. אֲבָל תַּלְמִידָיו שֶׁל בִּלְעָם הָרָשָׁע יוֹרְשִׁין גֵּיהִנָּם וְיוֹרְדִין לִבְאֵר שַׁחַת, שֶׁנֶּאֱמַר: וְאַתָּה אֱלֹהִים תּוֹרִדֵם לִבְאֵר שַׁחַת, אַנְשֵׁי דָמִים וּמִרְמָה לֹא יֶחֱצוּ יְמֵיהֶם, וַאֲנִי אֶבְטַח בָּךְ.

---

rat Chaim, Vayera 114b; Mili d'Chasiduta).

Evil eye. As a person perceives his enemy, an evil eye perceives only evil even in the good deeds of others (ibid.).

Balaam. Balaam was a prophet who sought to curse the Israelites in the desert. When he failed to curse them, he enticed them to sin and thereby brought a plague upon them (see Numbers 22:2).

Balaam epitomizes hedonism and dominance of body over soul. Abraham epitomizes the dominance of soul over body and the sanctification of the physical (Maharal).

The disciples of Abraham…eat in this

world…the World to Come. They interact with the physical in a sanctified way, such that they inherit the World to Come (see Chatam Sofer).

Shall not live out half their days. The condition of the physical is gradual deterioration. Those who are subservient to the physical, deteriorate faster than those who live more spiritual lives. Indeed Balaam died at age 33—less then half of his days (see Psalms 90:10: "The years of our life number seventy…"; Maharal; Sanhedrin 106b).

But I will trust in you. Although there are treacherous men—disciples of Balaam—in the world, I shall not fear, since I trust in You (Biurim).

through him; but anyone who causes the masses to sin shall not be granted the opportunity to repent. Moshe was himself meritorious and caused the masses to attain merit, [therefore] the merit of the masses are attributed to him, as it says: *He (Moshe) performed the righteousness of G-d and His ordinances together with Israel.*[26] Jeroboam son of Nevat sinned himself and caused the masses to sin, [therefore] the sins of the masses are attributed to him, as it says: *For the sins of Jeroboam that he sinned and caused Israel to sin.*[27]

19. Anyone who possesses the following three characteristics is of the disciples of Abraham our father; and [anyone who possesses] three other characteristics, is of the disciples of Balaam the wicked. The disciples of our father Abraham possess a generous eye, a humble spirit, and a modest soul. The disciples of Balaam the wicked possess an evil eye, an arrogant spirit, and a gluttonous soul.

What is the difference between the disciples of Abraham our father and the disciples of the wicked Balaam? The disciples of Abraham our father eat [enjoy the fruits of their good qualities] in this world and inherit the World to Come, as it says: *To cause those who love Me to inherit an everlasting possession [i.e., the World to Come], and I will fill their storehouses [in this world].*[28] But the disciples of Balaam the wicked inherit Purgatory and descend into the nethermost pit, as it says: *And You, O G-d, will bring them down to the nethermost pit; bloodthirsty and treacherous men shall not live out half their days; but I will trust in You.*[29]

Shall not be granted the opportunity to repent. "He should not be in Paradise while his students are in Purgatory" (ibid.). Although the gates of repentance are never closed, Heaven does not assist him in finding repentance (*Tiferet Yisrael*; see *Tanya* ch. 25).

Jeroboam. Jeroboam, who became king of ten Israelite tribes after King Solomon's passing, led his subjects into idolatry (see I Kings 15:30).

19. Generous eye. As a father perceives his only child, a generous eye perceives only good in others (see *To-*

---

26. Deuteronomy 33:21.   27. I Kings 15:30.   28. Proverbs 8:21. Cf. Uktzin 3:12.   29. Psalms 55:24.

כ. יְהוּדָה בֶּן תֵּימָא אוֹמֵר: הֱוֵי עַז כַּנָּמֵר, וְקַל כַּנֶּשֶׁר, רָץ כַּצְּבִי, וְגִבּוֹר כָּאֲרִי, לַעֲשׂוֹת רְצוֹן אָבִיךָ שֶׁבַּשָּׁמָיִם. הוּא הָיָה אוֹמֵר: עַז פָּנִים לְגֵיהִנֹּם, וּבוֹשֶׁת פָּנִים לְגַן עֵדֶן. יְהִי רָצוֹן מִלְּפָנֶיךָ, יְיָ אֱלֹהֵינוּ וֵאלֹהֵי אֲבוֹתֵינוּ, שֶׁיִּבָּנֶה בֵּית הַמִּקְדָּשׁ בִּמְהֵרָה בְיָמֵינוּ, וְתֵן חֶלְקֵנוּ בְּתוֹרָתֶךָ.

כא. בֶּן בַּג בַּג אוֹמֵר: הֲפָךְ בָּהּ וַהֲפָךְ בָּהּ, דְּכֹלָּא בָהּ, וּבָהּ תֶּחֱזֵי, וְסִיב וּבְלֵה בָהּ, וּמִנַּהּ לָא תָזוּעַ, שֶׁאֵין לְךָ מִדָּה טוֹבָה הֵימֶנָּה. בֶּן הֵא הֵא אוֹמֵר: לְפוּם צַעֲרָא אַגְרָא.

כב. הוּא הָיָה אוֹמֵר: בֶּן חָמֵשׁ שָׁנִים לְמִקְרָא, בֶּן עֶשֶׂר שָׁנִים לְמִשְׁנָה, בֶּן שְׁלֹשׁ עֶשְׂרֵה לְמִצְוֹת, בֶּן חֲמֵשׁ עֶשְׂרֵה לִגְמָרָא, בֶּן שְׁמוֹנֶה עֶשְׂרֵה לְחֻפָּה, בֶּן עֶשְׂרִים לִרְדֹּף, בֶּן שְׁלֹשִׁים לְכֹחַ, בֶּן אַרְבָּעִים לְבִינָה, בֶּן חֲמִשִּׁים לְעֵצָה, בֶּן שִׁשִּׁים לְזִקְנָה, בֶּן

(fifth letter of the Hebrew alphabet) that were added to the names of Abraham and Sarah, the first "converts" to Judaism. בג (*Bet*=2, *Gimmel*=3) is numerically equivalent to ה (5) (*Midrash Shmuel*).

Everything is in it. The Torah is the blueprint for all of creation. Understanding the depths of Torah therefore leads to comprehension of all of creation (*Maharal*).

Additionally: "Everything," meaning all of Torah, "is in it," in every aspect of Torah. Every detail of Torah contains a microcosm of the entire Torah (*Biurim*; see below 6:3).

Pain...reward. Only through painstaking study of Torah can one perceive its spiritual depths. Only then can one see that "everything—every wisdom—is in it." But the pain is well worth the reward (*Sforno*).

22. He used to say. I.e., Yehudah ben Teima cited above Mishnah 20 (see *Biurim* fn. 534).

According to R.Y. ben Shlomo cited in *Midrash Shmuel*, these are not the words of Yehudah ben Teima nor were they originally part of *Avot*.

Twenty—pursuit [of a livelihood]. Twenty is the age to leave the cocoon of Torah study and bring its light to the world (see *Biurim*).

Maturity. *Ziknah* in Hebrew, which connotes "one who has acquired wisdom" (*Kiddushin* 32b). As the body weakens, the mind grows stronger. It can now perceive abstract concepts formerly beyond its grasp (*Maharal*; *Midrash Shmuel*).

20. Yehudah ben Teima said: Be brazen as a leopard, light as an eagle, swift as a deer, and strong as a lion, to fulfill the will of your Father in heaven. He used to say: The brazenfaced to Purgatory; the shamefaced to Paradise. May it be Your will, L-rd our G-d and G-d of our fathers, that the Holy Temple be rebuilt speedily in our days, and grant us our portion in Your Torah.

21. Ben Bag Bag said: Delve and delve into it [the Torah], for everything is in it; with it you will perceive. Grow old and worn over it, and do not stir from it, for you can have no better portion than it. Ben Hay Hay said: According to the pain is the reward.

22. He used to say: **Five** years is the age for the study of Scripture; **ten**—the study of Mishnah; **thirteen**—[the obligation to observe] the *mitzvot*; **fifteen**—the study of Talmud; **eighteen**—marriage; **twenty**—pursuit [of a livelihood]; **thirty**—full strength; **forty**—understanding; **fifty**—[the ability to offer] counsel; **sixty**—maturity; **seventy**—ripe old age; **eighty**

---

20. Brazen. Although brazenness is a negative trait, one should "borrow" it when necessary (*Rambam*), such as to do a mitzvah despite the mockery of cynics (*Tur*). But one should not *become* brazenfaced. When a person's brazenness is fueled solely by the desire "to fulfill the will of his Father in Heaven"—not by his ego—it bears no negative consequence (*Biurim*).

May...the Holy Temple be rebuilt. The Mishnah concludes with a prayer for the commencement of the Messianic era, when evil will be banished from the world, and the need to act brazenly—even for a holy purpose—will no longer exist (*Midrash Shmuel*).

Grant us our portion in your Torah.

And if our portion, i.e., our nature, contains negative traits, such as brazenness, help us to use it only for positive purposes—"in your Torah"—such as to be brazen and not to be ashamed to ask when we do not understand (*Midrash Shmuel*).

Similarly, grant us that our "portion," i.e., occupation, should be in your Torah. In the Messianic era (when the Temple will be rebuilt), man will no longer engage in mundane activities and will be entirely devoted to G-dly pursuits—our portion will be in Torah (*Biurim*).

21. Ben Bag Bag . . . Ben Hay Hay. Ben Bag Bag and Ben Hay Hay were converts to Judaism. They were called by these pseudonyms for their safety. Their names allude to the two *Hay*s

שִׁבְעִים לְשֵׂיבָה, בֶּן שְׁמוֹנִים לִגְבוּרָה, בֶּן תִּשְׁעִים לָשׁוּחַ, בֶּן מֵאָה כְּאִלּוּ מֵת וְעָבַר וּבָטֵל מִן הָעוֹלָם.

רַבִּי חֲנַנְיָא בֶּן עֲקַשְׁיָא אוֹמֵר: רָצָה הַקָּדוֹשׁ בָּרוּךְ הוּא לְזַכּוֹת אֶת יִשְׂרָאֵל, לְפִיכָךְ הִרְבָּה לָהֶם תּוֹרָה וּמִצְוֹת, שֶׁנֶּאֱמַר: יְיָ חָפֵץ לְמַעַן צִדְקוֹ, יַגְדִּיל תּוֹרָה וְיַאְדִּיר.

∽⤫⤫∽

world. As explained at the beginning of this chapter, the world was created with ten utterances. Everything in the world is therefore configured in units of ten. Accordingly, man's life is divided into ten units of ten (see *Maharal*).

One who lives a spiritually full life for one hundred years has reached a state of spiritual perfection. He is now "dead"—in a positive sense—freed from the limitations of an earthly consciousness.

He perceives reality with the perspective of one who has passed on to the World of Truth (*Biurim*; see *Chida, Zeroa Yemin*).

—strength; **ninety**—bending forward; **one hundred**—it is as if he were dead, passed away and ceased from the world.

Rabbi Chananyah ben Akashya said: The Holy One, blessed be He, wished to make Israel meritorious. He therefore increased for them Torah and mitzvot, as it says: *G-d desired, for the sake of his [Israel's] righteousness, to make the Torah great and glorious.*[30] (*Makkot* 3:16)

Ripe old age. At **seventy**—the end of the typical lifespan—one has lived a full life. One who reaches **eighty** has been blessed with an extra measure of strength from G-d (*Mefarshim*; Psalms 90:10) and is capable of achieving even greater perfection (see *Maharal*).

Ninety...bending forward. Even after his extensive achievements he remains humble. This humility causes his body to instinctively bend forward (*Biurim*).

One hundred...ceased from the

30. Isaiah 42:21.

כָּל יִשְׂרָאֵל יֵשׁ לָהֶם חֵלֶק לְעוֹלָם הַבָּא, שֶׁנֶּאֱמַר: וְעַמֵּךְ כֻּלָּם צַדִּיקִים, לְעוֹלָם יִירְשׁוּ אָרֶץ, נֵצֶר מַטָּעַי מַעֲשֵׂה יָדַי לְהִתְפָּאֵר.

א. שָׁנוּ חֲכָמִים בִּלְשׁוֹן הַמִּשְׁנָה, בָּרוּךְ שֶׁבָּחַר בָּהֶם וּבְמִשְׁנָתָם.

רַבִּי מֵאִיר אוֹמֵר: כָּל הָעוֹסֵק בַּתּוֹרָה לִשְׁמָהּ זוֹכֶה לִדְבָרִים הַרְבֵּה, וְלֹא עוֹד, אֶלָּא שֶׁכָּל הָעוֹלָם כֻּלּוֹ כְּדַאי הוּא לוֹ. נִקְרָא רֵעַ, אָהוּב, אוֹהֵב אֶת הַמָּקוֹם, אוֹהֵב אֶת הַבְּרִיּוֹת, מְשַׂמֵּחַ אֶת הַמָּקוֹם, מְשַׂמֵּחַ אֶת הַבְּרִיּוֹת, וּמַלְבַּשְׁתּוֹ עֲנָוָה וְיִרְאָה, וּמַכְשַׁרְתּוֹ לִהְיוֹת צַדִּיק, חָסִיד, יָשָׁר, וְנֶאֱמָן, וּמְרַחַקְתּוֹ מִן הַחֵטְא, וּמְקָרַבְתּוֹ לִידֵי זְכוּת, וְנֶהֱנִין מִמֶּנּוּ עֵצָה וְתוּשִׁיָּה, בִּינָה וּגְבוּרָה, שֶׁנֶּאֱמַר: לִי עֵצָה וְתוּשִׁיָּה, אֲנִי בִינָה, לִי גְבוּרָה, וְנוֹתֶנֶת לוֹ מַלְכוּת וּמֶמְשָׁלָה, וְחִקּוּר דִּין, וּמְגַלִּין לוֹ רָזֵי תוֹרָה, וְנַעֲשֶׂה כְּמַעְיָן הַמִּתְגַּבֵּר וּכְנָהָר שֶׁאֵינוֹ פוֹסֵק, וְהֹוֶה צָנוּעַ, וְאֶרֶךְ רוּחַ, וּמוֹחֵל עַל עֶלְבּוֹנוֹ, וּמְגַדַּלְתּוֹ וּמְרוֹמַמְתּוֹ עַל כָּל הַמַּעֲשִׂים.

ב. אָמַר רַבִּי יְהוֹשֻׁעַ בֶּן לֵוִי, בְּכָל יוֹם וָיוֹם בַּת קוֹל יוֹצֵאת מֵהַר חוֹרֵב וּמַכְרֶזֶת וְאוֹמֶרֶת: אוֹי לָהֶם לַבְּרִיּוֹת מֵעֶלְבּוֹנָהּ שֶׁל תּוֹרָה,

---

(*Bartenura*); but this fact should not diminish its worth in one's eyes, since it is "in the language of the Mishnah," i.e., its stature is nearly equal to those teachings included in the Mishnaic body (*Midrash Shmuel*).

For its own sake. I.e., to bind his soul to G-d through grasping Torah (*Tanya* ch. 5) not for any personal benefit—even the benefit of applying Torah in practice (see *Chatam Sofer Nedarim* 81a). The Mishnah informs this student that despite his abstract approach, the Torah will affect him practically—it will change his character, as the Mishnah elaborates. He

will merit many things that would otherwise require much effort and focus (see *Biurim*).

● For most individuals, it is difficult to study Torah for its own sake throughout an entire study session. However, one is considered to be studying "for its sake" if each study session is *begun* "for its sake" (*Biurim*; *Tanya* ch. 41).

2. Echo. This Heavenly voice from Horeb—i.e., Sinai—is heard by the soul, which in turn inspires man to return to Torah (*Maharal*). According to *Midrash Shmuel*, one should imagine Horeb proclaiming the above.

CHAPTER SIX

All of Israel have a share in the World to Come, as it says, *Your people are all righteous; they will inherit the Land forever; they are the branch of My planting, the work of My hands in which I take pride.*[1] (*Sanhedrin* 11:1)

---

1. *The Sages taught in the language of the Mishnah—blessed is He who chose them and their teachings:*

    R. Meir said: Whoever occupies himself with Torah for its own sake merits many things; not only that, the [creation of the] entire world is worthwhile for him alone. He is called "friend," "beloved"; he loves G-d, he loves mankind; he brings joy to G-d, he brings joy to mankind. [The Torah] garbs him with humility and fear [of G-d]; makes him fit to be righteous, pious, upright and faithful; keeps him far from sin and brings him close to merit. From him people enjoy counsel and wisdom, insight and strength, as it says: *Counsel and wisdom are mine; I am understanding, strength is mine.*[2] It bestows upon him royalty, authority and discerning judgment; the secrets of the Torah are revealed to him. He becomes like a fountain flowing with ever-increasing strength and like an unceasing stream. He becomes modest, patient, and forgiving of insult; it elevates him and exalts him above all things.

2. R. Yehoshua ben Levi said: Each and every day an echo goes forth from Mount Horeb, proclaiming and saying, "Woe is to

---

CHAPTER SIX. The following chapter (taken from a collection of Tannaic writings—called *beraitot*—that were not included in the Mishnah) was appended to the five chapters of Avot by the sages of the Talmud (*Lechem Shamayim*; see the 9th century *Siddur Rav Amram Gaon*).

• Chapter six speaks of the greatness of Torah and inspires its reader to

love and cherish the Torah. Appropriately, it is always read on the Shabbat before Shavuot, the holiday that celebrates the giving of the Torah (*Ha-Chasid*).

1. In the language of the Mishnah. I.e., Hebrew (unlike the Talmud, which is written in Aramaic). This phrase teaches that the following chapter is not part of the Mishnah

---

1. Isaiah 60:21.   2. Proverbs 8:14.

שֶׁכָּל מִי שֶׁאֵינוֹ עוֹסֵק בַּתּוֹרָה נִקְרָא נָזוּף, שֶׁנֶּאֱמַר: נֶזֶם זָהָב
בְּאַף חֲזִיר, אִשָּׁה יָפָה וְסָרַת טָעַם. וְאוֹמֵר: וְהַלֻּחֹת מַעֲשֵׂה
אֱלֹהִים הֵמָּה, וְהַמִּכְתָּב מִכְתַּב אֱלֹהִים הוּא, חָרוּת עַל הַלֻּחֹת,
אַל תִּקְרֵי חָרוּת אֶלָּא חֵרוּת, שֶׁאֵין לְךָ בֶּן חוֹרִין, אֶלָּא מִי
שֶׁעוֹסֵק בְּתַלְמוּד תּוֹרָה, וְכָל מִי שֶׁעוֹסֵק בְּתַלְמוּד תּוֹרָה, הֲרֵי
זֶה מִתְעַלֶּה, שֶׁנֶּאֱמַר: וּמִמַּתָּנָה נַחֲלִיאֵל, וּמִנַּחֲלִיאֵל בָּמוֹת.

ג. הַלּוֹמֵד מֵחֲבֵרוֹ פֶּרֶק אֶחָד, אוֹ הֲלָכָה אַחַת, אוֹ פָּסוּק אֶחָד, אוֹ
דִבּוּר אֶחָד, אוֹ אֲפִלּוּ אוֹת אַחַת, צָרִיךְ לִנְהֹג בּוֹ כָּבוֹד, שֶׁכֵּן
מָצִינוּ בְדָוִד מֶלֶךְ יִשְׂרָאֵל, שֶׁלֹּא לָמַד מֵאֲחִיתֹפֶל אֶלָּא שְׁנֵי
דְבָרִים בִּלְבָד, קְרָאוֹ רַבּוֹ אַלּוּפוֹ וּמְיֻדָּעוֹ, שֶׁנֶּאֱמַר: וְאַתָּה אֱנוֹשׁ
כְּעֶרְכִּי, אַלּוּפִי וּמְיֻדָּעִי. וַהֲלֹא דְבָרִים קַל וָחֹמֶר, וּמַה דָּוִד מֶלֶךְ
יִשְׂרָאֵל שֶׁלֹּא לָמַד מֵאֲחִיתֹפֶל אֶלָּא שְׁנֵי דְבָרִים בִּלְבָד, קְרָאוֹ

Free. Torah helps a person temper his involvement in the physical so that he does not become enslaved to it (see *Midrash Shmuel*).

● The natural desire of the soul is to serve G-d. Hence, if a person's life is not consistent with Torah, he enslaves the soul. Only a life consistent with Torah sets the soul free (*Biurim*).

From Mattanah. In its literal context, the verse refers to the travels of the Israelites in the desert: from a place called *Mattanah* to a place called *Nachaliel*, etc. (Numbers 21:19). Our Mishnah offers a homiletic interpretation of these names: the Torah is a *gift* that grants its student a *G-dly inheritance* that *elevates* him beyond the temporal (see *R. Moshe Almoshnino, Biurim*).

3. Only two things from Achitophel. Achitophel, a great Torah scholar and royal advisor, turned against David and advised David's son Absalom to rebel.

He taught David that one should not study alone and that one should not enter the study hall with an erect, arrogant posture (*Rashi*).

● The infinite nature of Torah is present in each of its teachings (see above 5:21). Every Torah teaching multiplies within its student into myriad insights and inspirations. But when a teaching is transmitted by an evil person like Achitophel, it becomes infertile. Hence the *Baraita's* logic: If David honored Achitophel for two "infertile" teachings, certainly one should honor a decent person for one teaching, since that teaching will multiply into many others (*Baal Shem Tov* in *Keter Shem Tov*, 22).

Others explain the logic as follows: If David, a *tzaddik* and king, honored the wicked and inferior Achitophel, surely one should honor an equal from whom one has learned (*Rashi*).

the people because of [their] affront to the Torah!" For whoever does not occupy himself with Torah is called "in contempt," as it says: *[Like] a golden ring in a swine's snout is a beautiful woman who lacks discretion.*[3] And it is further stated: *The Tablets were the work of G-d, and the writing was the writing of G-d,* charut *(engraved) on the Tablets.*[4] Do not read *charut* but *cherut* (freedom), for there is no free man except one who occupies himself with the study of Torah; and anyone who occupies himself with the study of Torah becomes elevated, as it says: *From Mattanah* ["the gift of Torah"] *to Nachaliel* ["the heritage of G-d"], *and from Nachaliel to Bamot* ["high places"].[5]

3. He who learns from his fellow a single chapter, a single Torah law, a single verse, a single [Biblical or Rabbinic] statement, or even a single letter, must show him honor. For so we find concerning David, King of Israel, who learned from Achitophel only two things, yet he called him his teacher, his guide, and his mentor, as it says: *You are a man equal to me; you are my guide and my mentor.*[6] Surely an *a fortiori* logic can be applied: If David, King of Israel, who learned only two things from Achitophel and yet

---

Like a golden ring.... The Mishnah uses beauty as a metaphor for the intellect. If the intellect is not employed for Divine wisdom, its beauty is wasted and ruined. Like the golden ring in the snout of a swine, this person's wisdom is enslaved to the material and buried in earthliness (*Maharal*).

Engraved. After mentioning the disadvantage of one who does not study Torah, the Mishnah turns to the advantage of one who does (see *Midrash Shmuel*).

Unlike letters of ink—which are separate from the parchment upon which they are written—letters engraved on stone are part of the stone.

One who internalizes Torah to such an extent that he is one with Torah is truly free. He is not subservient to any emotional or physical needs —rather, he makes his entire reality a part of his Divine service (*Biurim*).

● The letters on the tablets were engraved through and through. They consisted entirely of form. Form, unlike matter, is not subject to deterioration and manipulation. Similarly, Torah is an abstract wisdom —"form"— that exists independent from its physical manifestation. One who attaches himself to Torah is therefore freed from the limitations of matter and materiality (*Maharal*).

---

3. Proverbs 11:22.　4. Exodus 32:16.　5. Numbers 21:19.　6. Psalms 55:14.

רַבּוֹ אַלּוּפוֹ וּמְיֻדָּעוֹ, הַלּוֹמֵד מֵחֲבֵרוֹ פֶּרֶק אֶחָד, אוֹ הֲלָכָה אַחַת,
אוֹ פָסוּק אֶחָד, אוֹ דִבּוּר אֶחָד, אוֹ אֲפִילוּ אוֹת אַחַת, עַל אַחַת
כַּמָּה וְכַמָּה שֶׁצָּרִיךְ לִנְהָג בּוֹ כָּבוֹד. וְאֵין כָּבוֹד אֶלָּא תוֹרָה,
שֶׁנֶּאֱמַר: כָּבוֹד חֲכָמִים יִנְחָלוּ, וּתְמִימִים יִנְחֲלוּ טוֹב. וְאֵין טוֹב
אֶלָּא תוֹרָה, שֶׁנֶּאֱמַר: כִּי לֶקַח טוֹב נָתַתִּי לָכֶם, תּוֹרָתִי אַל תַּעֲזֹבוּ.

ד. כַּךְ הִיא דַרְכָּהּ שֶׁל תּוֹרָה: פַּת בְּמֶלַח תֹּאכֵל, וּמַיִם בִּמְשׂוּרָה
תִשְׁתֶּה, וְעַל הָאָרֶץ תִּישָׁן, וְחַיֵּי צַעַר תִּחְיֶה, וּבַתּוֹרָה אַתָּה עָמֵל,
אִם אַתָּה עוֹשֶׂה כֵן, אַשְׁרֶיךָ וְטוֹב לָךְ, אַשְׁרֶיךָ בָּעוֹלָם הַזֶּה, וְטוֹב
לָךְ לָעוֹלָם הַבָּא.

ה. אַל תְּבַקֵּשׁ גְּדֻלָּה לְעַצְמְךָ, וְאַל תַּחְמוֹד כָּבוֹד, יוֹתֵר מִלִּמּוּדְךָ
עֲשֵׂה, וְאַל תִּתְאַוֶּה לְשֻׁלְחָנָם שֶׁל מְלָכִים, שֶׁשֻּׁלְחָנְךָ גָּדוֹל
מִשֻּׁלְחָנָם, וְכִתְרְךָ גָּדוֹל מִכִּתְרָם, וְנֶאֱמָן הוּא בַּעַל מְלַאכְתֶּךָ
שֶׁיְּשַׁלֶּם לְךָ שְׂכַר פְּעֻלָּתֶךָ.

ו. גְּדוֹלָה תוֹרָה יוֹתֵר מִן הַכְּהֻנָּה וּמִן הַמַּלְכוּת, שֶׁהַמַּלְכוּת נִקְנֵית
בִּשְׁלֹשִׁים מַעֲלוֹת, וְהַכְּהֻנָּה בְּעֶשְׂרִים וְאַרְבַּע, וְהַתּוֹרָה נִקְנֵית

---

or unnecessary remark (see *Igrot Kodesh* 13:465).

5. Do not seek greatness for yourself.
Do not seek greatness for *yourself*, i.e., for your own benefit and prestige; but you may do so for the sake of the community (*Midrash Shmuel*).

• *Notzer Chesed* offers this interpretation: "Do not seek the great expansiveness, vitality, light, and sweetness of Torah and *mitzvot*. Although there is no greater pleasure or joy in the world that exceeds the spiritual delight of Torah, prayer and *mitzvot*, nevertheless, do it all for the sake of the Creator, to give pleasure before Him, blessed be He."

Do not covet honor. Obviously you should not actively *seek* honor; in ad-dition, you should not even covet it in your heart (*Biurim*). Study Torah solely for its own sake (*Bartenura*).

Let your deeds exceed your learning.
Force yourself to do and study more than you are naturally inclined (*Zechut Avot, Biurim*).

6. Thirty distinctions of royalty.
Such as: the restrictions on civilians in regard to riding upon the king's horse, sitting upon his throne, using his scepter, etc. (see I Samuel ch. 8 and Sanhedrin ch. 2.; see *Bartenura, Notzer Chesed*). According to *Abarbanel*, the thirty distinctions include such requirements as: appointment by a prophet, a court of seventy-one judges and anointment with special oil in Jerusalem (*Meam Loez*).

called him his teacher, his guide, and his mentor—one who learns from his peer a single chapter, a single Torah law, a single verse, a single statement, or even a single letter, how much more ought he treat him with honor! And honor is due only for Torah, as it says: *The wise shall inherit honor*[7] *. . . and the perfect shall inherit good.*[8] And [true] good is only Torah, as it says: *I have given you a good Teaching; do not forsake My Torah.*[9]

4. Such is the way of Torah: Eat bread with salt and drink water in small measure, sleep on the ground and live a life of austerity—and in the Torah you shall toil. If you do this, *you shall be happy, and it shall be well with you:*[10] *"You shall be happy"* in this world; *"and it shall be well with you"*—in the World to Come.

5. Do not seek greatness for yourself, and do not covet honor. Let your deeds exceed your learning. And do not crave the table of kings, for your table is greater than their table and your crown is greater than their crown; and faithful is He, the Master of your labor, that He will pay you the reward for your work.

6. Torah is greater than priesthood and royalty. For royalty is acquired with thirty distinctions, and the priesthood with

---

4. **The way of Torah**. This passage addresses a pauper who cannot afford anything more than the bare minimum, who must sleep on the ground for lack of a bed. He should nevertheless continue to study Torah and in the end will be blessed with physical and spiritual wealth (*Bartenura*). Additionally, even one who can afford to live well should live an austere life. This will enable him to devote more time to spiritual matters (*Sforno*) and will condition him for the sublime spirituality of Torah (see *Maharal*). According to *Chida*, the *beraita* is not advocating asceticism. Rather, the way of Torah is such that one should be so absorbed in its study that one is oblivious to all physical desires (*Petach Einayim*).

● Beginning with the Baal Shem Tov, the Chasidic masters strongly discouraged fasting and other forms of self-flagellation. People have grown weaker and can no longer function well while maintaining such practices. "A small hole in the body creates a large hole in the soul," said the Maggid of Mezritch (*Hatamim*, p. 664). One who insists on practicing self-affliction should do so in ways that do not weaken the body, for example: resisting the urge to make a negative

---

7. Proverbs 3:35.   8. Ibid. 28:10.   9. Ibid. 4:2.   10. Psalms 128:2.

בְּאַרְבָּעִים וּשְׁמוֹנָה דְבָרִים. וְאֵלוּ הֵן: בַּתַּלְמוּד, בִּשְׁמִיעַת הָאֹזֶן,
בַּעֲרִיכַת שְׂפָתַיִם, בְּבִינַת הַלֵּב, בְּאֵימָה, בְּיִרְאָה, בַּעֲנָוָה, בְּשִׂמְחָה,
בְּטָהֳרָה, בְּשִׁמּוּשׁ חֲכָמִים, בְּדִבּוּק חֲבֵרִים, בְּפִלְפּוּל הַתַּלְמִידִים,
בְּיִשּׁוּב, בְּמִקְרָא, בְּמִשְׁנָה, בְּמִעוּט סְחוֹרָה, בְּמִעוּט דֶּרֶךְ אֶרֶץ,
בְּמִעוּט תַּעֲנוּג, בְּמִעוּט שֵׁנָה, בְּמִעוּט שִׂיחָה, בְּמִעוּט שְׂחוֹק, בְּאֶרֶךְ
אַפַּיִם, בְּלֵב טוֹב, בֶּאֱמוּנַת חֲכָמִים, בְּקַבָּלַת הַיִּסּוּרִין, הַמַּכִּיר אֶת
מְקוֹמוֹ, וְהַשָּׂמֵחַ בְּחֶלְקוֹ, וְהָעוֹשֶׂה סְיָג לִדְבָרָיו, וְאֵינוֹ מַחֲזִיק
טוֹבָה לְעַצְמוֹ, אָהוּב, אוֹהֵב אֶת הַמָּקוֹם, אוֹהֵב אֶת הַבְּרִיּוֹת, אוֹהֵב
אֶת הַצְּדָקוֹת, אוֹהֵב אֶת הַמֵּישָׁרִים, אוֹהֵב אֶת הַתּוֹכָחוֹת, וּמִתְרַחֵק
מִן הַכָּבוֹד, וְלֹא מֵגִיס לִבּוֹ בְּתַלְמוּדוֹ, וְאֵינוֹ שָׂמֵחַ בְּהוֹרָאָה, נוֹשֵׂא
בְעוֹל עִם חֲבֵרוֹ, וּמַכְרִיעוֹ לְכַף זְכוּת, וּמַעֲמִידוֹ עַל הָאֱמֶת,
וּמַעֲמִידוֹ עַל הַשָּׁלוֹם, וּמִתְיַשֵּׁב לִבּוֹ בְּתַלְמוּדוֹ, שׁוֹאֵל וּמֵשִׁיב,

---

grasp of Torah and ability to re-
member it (*Maharal*; *Eiruvin* 54a).

Meditation of the heart. I.e., de-
voting his heart and mind to his studies and understanding it well in his
heart (*Maharal*). "If he applies his
heart to understand, he will understand what was placed in his heart at
Sinai, since every soul returns and re-
members what it received" (*Meam
Loez*).

Awe…fear. One acquires awe of G-d
by contemplating His awesomeness;
one attains fear of G-d by contemplating man's insignificance (*Maharal*).

One who knows his place. At this
point the *beraita* begins to list the
qualities differently. Whereas the first
twenty-four qualities are prefaced
with "with" (*with* study, *with* attentive listening, etc.), from this point
on each quality is conveyed by de-

scribing the individual, "one who
knows his place," etc.

R. Moshe Almoshnino explains that
one *acquires* Torah with the first
twenty-four qualities and *retains* the
Torah through the latter twenty-four
(*Midrash Shmuel*). According to *Lechem Shamayim*, the latter twenty-
four qualities are the practical man-
ifestations of the first. E.g., one who
acquires humility will know his place;
one who acquires a good heart will be
happy with his lot, etc.

A fence around his words. He carefully considers his words before
speaking (*Maharal*).

Bears the burden. If his friend suffers
some misfortune, he will help out and
carry the burden with him (*Maharal*).

Asks and responds. He asks questions
when he does not understand and
graciously answers the questions of
others when he can (*Maharal*).

twenty-four, whereas the Torah is acquired with forty-eight qualities. They are the following: with [constant] study, with attentive listening, with verbal enunciation, with meditation of the heart, with awe, with fear, with modesty, with joy, with purity, with ministering to sages, with the bonding of friends, with sharp discussion with students, with calmness, with [knowledge of] Scripture, with [knowledge of] Mishnah, with minimized business activity, with minimized worldly activity, with minimized pleasure, with minimized sleep, with minimized conversation, with minimized laughter, with slowness to anger, with goodness of heart, with faith in the Sages, with acceptance of suffering, one who knows his place, and one who is happy with his lot, and one who makes a fence around his words, he claims no credit for his achievements, he is loved, loves God, loves humanity, loves the ways of righteousness, loves justice, loves reproof, and keeps far from honor, and does not act arrogantly with his knowledge, and does not take pleasure in handing down [halachic] decisions, bears the burden with his friend, and judges him favorably, and places him in [the path of] truth, and places him in [the path of] peace, he deliberates in his study, asks and responds, listens and adds, one who learns in order to teach, and

---

Twenty-four. These refer to the twenty-four types of gifts the priests receive, such as various parts of the offerings, the firstborn animals, the first fruits, the first shearings and other gifts (see *Bartenura*; *Bava Kama* 110b).

Chida cites "an early manuscript" according to which the 24 distinctions refer to certain prerequisites, such as: holiness, purity, distinguished dress, frequent grooming, ritual purity, restrictions on suitable mates, and lack of physical defects (*Petach Einayim*).

● **Priesthood and Royalty.** In addition to its literal meaning, the priesthood and royalty mentioned here refer also to the "priesthood" and "royalty" that the Torah bestows upon its student: priesthood in the sense of spiritual transcendence, and royalty in the sense of sovereignty over the physical. Thus, the *beraita* instructs the student to study Torah for its own sake, not for the "priesthood" and "royalty" it confers. For Torah itself surpasses the "priesthood" and "royalty" that are its byproducts (*Biurim*).

Verbal enunciation. I.e., audibly pronouncing words of Torah as opposed to simply thinking Torah thoughts. Verbal enunciation improves one's

שׁוֹמֵעַ וּמוֹסִיף, הַלּוֹמֵד עַל מְנָת לְלַמֵּד, וְהַלּוֹמֵד עַל מְנָת לַעֲשׂוֹת,
הַמַּחְכִּים אֶת רַבּוֹ, וְהַמְכַוֵּן אֶת שְׁמוּעָתוֹ, וְהָאוֹמֵר דָּבָר בְּשֵׁם
אוֹמְרוֹ, הָא לָמַדְתָּ, כָּל הָאוֹמֵר דָּבָר בְּשֵׁם אוֹמְרוֹ, מֵבִיא גְאֻלָּה
לָעוֹלָם, שֶׁנֶּאֱמַר: וַתֹּאמֶר אֶסְתֵּר לַמֶּלֶךְ בְּשֵׁם מָרְדְּכָי.

ז. גְּדוֹלָה תוֹרָה, שֶׁהִיא נוֹתֶנֶת חַיִּים לְעֹשֶׂיהָ בָּעוֹלָם הַזֶּה
וּבָעוֹלָם הַבָּא, שֶׁנֶּאֱמַר: כִּי חַיִּים הֵם לְמוֹצְאֵיהֶם, וּלְכָל בְּשָׂרוֹ
מַרְפֵּא. וְאוֹמֵר: רִפְאוּת תְּהִי לְשָׁרֶּךָ, וְשִׁקּוּי לְעַצְמוֹתֶיךָ. וְאוֹמֵר:
עֵץ חַיִּים הִיא לַמַּחֲזִיקִים בָּהּ, וְתֹמְכֶיהָ מְאֻשָּׁר. וְאוֹמֵר: כִּי
לִוְיַת חֵן הֵם לְרֹאשֶׁךָ, וַעֲנָקִים לְגַרְגְּרֹתֶיךָ. וְאוֹמֵר: תִּתֵּן
לְרֹאשְׁךָ לִוְיַת חֵן, עֲטֶרֶת תִּפְאֶרֶת תְּמַגְּנֶךָּ. וְאוֹמֵר: כִּי בִי יִרְבּוּ

---

necessarily immediate or complete. In fact, the example offered by the *beraita*, that of Esther citing Mordechai, took place long before the redemption from Haman. Moreover, that redemption was not complete, since we still do not possess self-rule (*Biurim*).

Esther told the king. When Mordechai overheard two officers plotting to kill the king, he reported it to Esther who relayed the information to the king in Mordechai's name. The Scroll of Esther mentions that it was *Esther* who reported the matter to the king —a seemingly irrelevant detail— in order to explain why she merited being the conduit of the Purim redemption (*Maharal*). [Alternatively, the fact that Esther credited Mordechai led ultimately to the downfall of Haman and the ensuing redemption.]

7. Gives life. This Mishnah emphasizes the greatness of Torah over *mitzvot*. Fulfillment of *mitzvot* that is not informed and illuminated by knowledge of Torah—the reasons for the *mitzvot*—is lifeless and dry. Torah study injects life and vitality into one

who practices the *mitzvot* (*Biurim*).

● According to *Maharal*, each one of the proof texts cited in the *beraita* emphasizes a different aspect of life granted by Torah:

A healing to all his flesh: This verse speaks of a healing for the *flesh*, the external part of the person, emphasizing Torah's effect on the most external aspects of the individual.

A remedy to your body: This verse speaks of the body and the bones, emphasizing the Torah's effect on the internal aspects of one's physical self.

A tree of life: This verse emphasizes *length* of physical life, the tree being the symbol of longevity.

A garland of grace for your head: This verse speaks of the *spiritual* life granted by Torah to the soul, which resides in the head (see *Tanya* ch. 9).

A crown of glory: This verse speaks of a more transcendent level of spiritual life symbolized by the crown, which transcends the head. (It also makes no mention of the neck, the source of

one who learns in order to practice, one who increases the wisdom of his teacher, and one who properly understands the meaning of what he learns, and one who relates a statement in the name of the one who said it. Indeed, you have learned: Whoever relates a statement in the name of the one who said it brings redemption to the world, as it says: *And Esther told the king in the name of Mordechai.*[11]

7. Torah is greater for it gives life to those who practice it—in this world and in the World to Come, as it says: *For they [the teachings of the Torah] are life to one who finds them, and a healing to all his flesh.*[12] It further says: *It shall be a remedy to your body and marrow to your bones.*[13] It further says: *It is a tree of life to those who hold fast to it, and fortunate are those who support it.*[14] It further says: *They are a garland of grace for your head and a necklace for your neck.*[15] It further says: *It will give to your head a garland of grace, a crown of glory it will bestow upon you.*[16] It further says: In-

---

In the name of the one who said it. If a person internalizes a teaching and it becomes "his own" he is no longer *required* to cite its original author. Nevertheless, the *beraita* instructs the student of Torah to go beyond the letter of the law and cite the original author (*Biurim*).

• Citing the original author of a Torah teaching emphasizes the chain of tradition, which links back to the reception of Torah by Moshe at Sinai (*Biurim*).

Brings redemption. When a person accustoms himself to recognizing the origin of things, including the Divine origin of Torah itself, he reveals the origin of everything in the world —the Divine utterance that brings it into being. He thereby *redeems* the

world from its state of Divine concealment (*Biurim*).

Similarly, by crediting Mordechai, Esther demonstrated her ability to recognize the source of a thing. She was therefore fit to bring G-d's redemption to the people, since she would not take the credit for herself but would attribute the redemption to G-d's supernatural intervention (*Maharal*).

• Citing the original author is one of the qualities through which the Torah is acquired because it brings the redemption of the world closer. And it is only then, when the earth will be filled with knowledge of G-d, that one will truly be capable of acquiring Torah (*Midrash Shmuel*).

Redemption. Any salvation from misfortune is considered a redemption (*Maharal*). This redemption is not

---

11. Esther 2:22.   12. Proverbs 4:22.   13. Ibid. 3:8.   14. Ibid. 3:18.   15. Ibid. 1:9.   16. Ibid. 4:9.

יָמֶיךָ, וְיוֹסִיפוּ לְךָ שְׁנוֹת חַיִּים. וְאוֹמֵר: אֹרֶךְ יָמִים בִּימִינָהּ,
בִּשְׂמֹאלָהּ עֹשֶׁר וְכָבוֹד. וְאוֹמֵר: כִּי אֹרֶךְ יָמִים וּשְׁנוֹת חַיִּים
וְשָׁלוֹם יוֹסִיפוּ לָךְ.

ח. רַבִּי שִׁמְעוֹן בֶּן יְהוּדָה מִשּׁוּם רַבִּי שִׁמְעוֹן בֶּן יוֹחַאי אוֹמֵר:
הַנּוֹי, וְהַכֹּחַ, וְהָעֹשֶׁר, וְהַכָּבוֹד, וְהַחָכְמָה, וְהַזִּקְנָה, וְהַשֵּׂיבָה,
וְהַבָּנִים, נָאֶה לַצַּדִּיקִים וְנָאֶה לָעוֹלָם, שֶׁנֶּאֱמַר: עֲטֶרֶת תִּפְאֶרֶת
שֵׂיבָה, בְּדֶרֶךְ צְדָקָה תִּמָּצֵא. וְאוֹמֵר: תִּפְאֶרֶת בַּחוּרִים כֹּחָם,
וַהֲדַר זְקֵנִים שֵׂיבָה. וְאוֹמֵר: עֲטֶרֶת זְקֵנִים בְּנֵי בָנִים, וְתִפְאֶרֶת
בָּנִים אֲבוֹתָם. וְאוֹמֵר: וְחָפְרָה הַלְּבָנָה וּבוֹשָׁה הַחַמָּה, כִּי מָלַךְ
יְיָ צְבָאוֹת בְּהַר צִיּוֹן וּבִירוּשָׁלַיִם, וְנֶגֶד זְקֵנָיו כָּבוֹד. רַבִּי
שִׁמְעוֹן בֶּן מְנַסְיָא אוֹמֵר: אֵלּוּ שֶׁבַע מִדּוֹת שֶׁמָּנוּ חֲכָמִים
לַצַּדִּיקִים, כֻּלָּם נִתְקַיְּמוּ בְּרַבִּי וּבְבָנָיו.

---

the righteous, since they enable them to be more persuasive conveyors of Divine wisdom to those around them (*Biurim*).

Beauty. A handsome person is in a better position to influence others. One who seeks to influence the world for the better should therefore take care that his appearance is pleasing (*Meiri; Biurim*).

Good for the world. The righteous person might yearn to be free of the distractions caused by these qualities—the temptations of beauty, the arrogance of honor, the disturbances of wealth, etc. The *beraita*, however, assures him that these qualities will not ruin him—*they are good for him*. Furthermore, he has no right to relinquish them, since *they are good for the world*—he possesses them for the world's benefit (*Biurim*).

Old age...ripe old age. *Old age* refers to the maturity gained through study;

ripe old age refers to the quality of equanimity and composure (*Biurim*).

Children. This can also refer to the quality of attracting students, since, like children who perpetuate the legacy of parents, students perpetuate the legacy of their teachers for future generations (*Biurim*).

Crown of beauty.... *Crown* indicates wealth. Wisdom is indicated by the Hebrew term for *old age*, which connotes "one who acquired wisdom" (*Bartenura*).

These seven qualities. Although the *beraita* lists eight things, it refers to seven qualities because "children" are not counted as a quality (*Biurim*).

All were realized in Rabbi and his sons. Although Rabbi and his sons possessed *all* of these qualities and their accompanying temptations, their spiritual stature was not lessened (*Biurim*).

• The author of this *beraita* seeks to

deed, through me [the Torah] your days shall be increased, and years of life shall be added to you.[17] It further says: *Length of days is at its right, riches and honor at its left.*[18] It further says: *Length of days, years of life, and peace shall they add to you.*[19]

8. R. Shimon ben Yehudah said in the name of R. Shimon ben Yochai: Beauty, strength, wealth, honor, wisdom, old age, ripe old age, and children, are good for the righteous and [when possessed by the righteous] good for the world, as it says: *Ripe old age is a crown of beauty, it is to be found in the path of righteousness.*[20] It further says: *The beauty of young men is their strength, and the splendor of the elders is ripe old age.*[21] It further says: *Grandchildren are the crown of the aged, and the glory of children are their fathers.*[22] It further says: *The moon shall be abashed and the sun put to shame when G-d of hosts will reign on Mount Zion and in Jerusalem, and honor shall be before His elders.*[23] R. Shimon ben Menasya said: These seven qualities which the Sages enumerated [as good for] the righteous—all of them were realized in Rabbi [Yehudah the Prince] and in his sons.

---

speech, which is a more physical attribute.)

Your days shall be increased: This verse is not cited in *Maharal's* version of the Mishnah and he does not comment on it. [Perhaps an *increase* in days and *added* years are a lower level than the *length* of days mentioned in the next verse. See next comment.]

Length of days: This verse emphasizes the *longevity* of spiritual life in the World to Come granted by Torah.

Years of life: *Years* of life surpasses length of *days*, and symbolizes *eternal* spiritual life, which is granted by Torah.

● The first three verses speak of the life granted by Torah in this world, while the last three verses speak of life in the World to Come. The fourth and middle verse is the bridge between them and alludes to both the spiritual, the head, and the physical, the neck, which is the source of speech (*Maharal*).

8. The eight qualities described in the *beraita* are neutral qualities. They enhance the righteous and become tools for the betterment of the world in their hands. In the hands of the wicked, however, they can harm theirs and the world's well-being (*Mefarshim*).

These qualities increase a person's prestige and are therefore befitting

---

17. Ibid. 9:11.   18. Ibid. 3:16.   19. Ibid. 3:2.   20. Ibid. 16:31.   21. Ibid. 20:29.   22. Ibid. 17:6.
23. Isaiah 24:23.

ט. אָמַר רַבִּי יוֹסֵי בֶּן קִסְמָא: פַּעַם אַחַת הָיִיתִי מְהַלֵּךְ בַּדֶּרֶךְ, וּפָגַע בִּי אָדָם אֶחָד, וְנָתַן לִי שָׁלוֹם, וְהֶחֱזַרְתִּי לוֹ: שָׁלוֹם, אָמַר לִי: רַבִּי, מֵאֵיזֶה מָקוֹם אָתָּה, אָמַרְתִּי לוֹ מֵעִיר גְּדוֹלָה שֶׁל חֲכָמִים וְשֶׁל סוֹפְרִים אָנִי. אָמַר לִי: רַבִּי, רְצוֹנְךָ שֶׁתָּדוּר עִמָּנוּ בִּמְקוֹמֵנוּ, וַאֲנִי אֶתֵּן לְךָ אֶלֶף אֲלָפִים דִּנְרֵי זָהָב וַאֲבָנִים טוֹבוֹת וּמַרְגָּלִיּוֹת. אָמַרְתִּי לוֹ: אִם אַתָּה נוֹתֵן לִי כָּל כֶּסֶף וְזָהָב וַאֲבָנִים טוֹבוֹת וּמַרְגָּלִיּוֹת שֶׁבָּעוֹלָם, אֵינִי דָר אֶלָּא בִּמְקוֹם תּוֹרָה, וְכֵן כָּתוּב בְּסֵפֶר תְּהִלִּים עַל יְדֵי דָוִד מֶלֶךְ יִשְׂרָאֵל: טוֹב לִי תוֹרַת פִּיךָ, מֵאַלְפֵי זָהָב וָכָסֶף. וְלֹא עוֹד, אֶלָּא שֶׁבִּשְׁעַת פְּטִירָתוֹ שֶׁל אָדָם, אֵין מְלַוִּין לוֹ לְאָדָם לֹא כֶסֶף וְלֹא זָהָב וְלֹא אֲבָנִים טוֹבוֹת וּמַרְגָּלִיּוֹת, אֶלָּא תוֹרָה וּמַעֲשִׂים טוֹבִים בִּלְבַד, שֶׁנֶּאֱמַר: בְּהִתְהַלֶּכְךָ תַּנְחֶה אֹתָךְ, בְּשָׁכְבְּךָ תִּשְׁמֹר עָלֶיךָ, וַהֲקִיצוֹתָ הִיא תְשִׂיחֶךָ. בְּהִתְהַלֶּכְךָ תַּנְחֶה אֹתָךְ, בָּעוֹלָם הַזֶּה. בְּשָׁכְבְּךָ תִּשְׁמֹר עָלֶיךָ, בַּקֶּבֶר. וַהֲקִיצוֹתָ הִיא תְשִׂיחֶךָ, לָעוֹלָם הַבָּא. וְאוֹמֵר: לִי הַכֶּסֶף וְלִי הַזָּהָב, נְאֻם יְיָ צְבָאוֹת.

י. חֲמִשָּׁה קִנְיָנִים קָנָה הַקָּדוֹשׁ בָּרוּךְ הוּא בְּעוֹלָמוֹ, וְאֵלוּ הֵן: תּוֹרָה,

---

position of *leader*, R. Yosay would have accepted (*Maharal*). Alternatively, the focus of R. Yosay's Divine service was Torah study. It was therefore inappropriate for *him* to live outside a place of Torah (*Biurim*).

David, King of Israel. King David possessed much gold and silver, which he certainly distributed to charity. Yet he said: *The Torah of Your mouth is more precious to me than thousands of gold and silver [coins]* (*Biurim*; see *Ktav Sofer*).

Silver...and gold is Mine. R. Yosay was therefore unimpressed with promises of wealth, since possession of silver and gold is in G-d's control: if He desires for me to have it, I will have it without your help; and if He does not wish me to have it, it will be futile for me to take it from you (*Midrash Shmuel*).

10. Acquisitions. Although all of creation belongs to G-d, this fact is not apparent. It requires effort to pierce through the façade of independent existence to reveal the face of G-d. But there are five entities in which G-d's ownership and presence is obvious.

An acquisition remains unchanged as it passes from one domain of ownership to another. Similarly, these five entities require no change in order to be united with G-d. The rest of creation, by contrast, requires change —the breaking down of its façade of independence—in order to reveal its unity with its Source:

9. R. Yosay ben Kisma said: Once I was walking on the road, when a certain man met me. He greeted me, "Shalom," and I returned his greeting, "Shalom." He said to me, "Rabbi, which place are you from?" I said to him, "I am from a great city of scholars and sages." He said to me, "Rabbi, do you wish to live with us in our place and I would give you a million golden *dinars*, precious stones and pearls?" I replied, "Even if you were to give me all the silver and gold, precious stones and pearls in the world, I would dwell nowhere but in a place of Torah." And so it is written in the Book of Psalms by David, King of Israel: *The Torah of Your mouth is more precious to me than thousands of gold and silver [coins].*[24] Furthermore, at the time of a man's passing from this world, neither silver nor gold nor precious stones nor pearls accompany him, but only Torah and good deeds, as it says: *When you walk, it [the Torah] shall guide you; when you lie down, it shall watch over you; and when you awake, it shall speak for you.*[25] *"When you walk, it shall guide you"*—in this world; *"when you lie down, it shall watch over you"*—in the grave; *"and when you awake, it shall speak for you"*—in the World to Come. It further says: *Silver is Mine, and gold is Mine, says the G-d of hosts.*[26]

10. Five acquisitions did the Holy One, blessed be He, acquire in His

---

indicate that *anyone* can attain *all* of these qualities. He therefore uses his contemporary Rabbi Yehudah—not an earlier sage or prophet—as an example of one who attained them (see *Sforno*). Rabbi's children are also mentioned in order to suggest that simply being Rabbi's "child,"—i.e., his student—enables one to attain these qualities (*Biurim*).

9. He greeted me. R. Yosay was so engrossed in Torah study that he did not notice the man until after he was greeted. Otherwise, he would have greeted the man first, in fulfillment of the dictum (above 4:15),

"be first to greet every person" (*Midrash Shmuel*).

A million golden dinars. R. Yosay would then be free to devote himself completely to Torah study and would possess much money with which to perform the mitzvah of charity (*Midrash Shmuel*). Yet he said:

I would dwell nowhere but in a place of Torah. R. Yosay refused the man's offer because the man intimated that R. Yosay would be welcome as an advisor, subordinate to the community—"come *live with us, in our place.*" Had the man offered him the

---

24. Psalms 119:72.   25. Proverbs 6:22. V. Rashi, loc. Cit.   26. Haggai 2:8.

קִנְיָן אֶחָד. שָׁמַיִם וָאָרֶץ, קִנְיָן אֶחָד. אַבְרָהָם, קִנְיָן אֶחָד. יִשְׂרָאֵל, קִנְיָן אֶחָד. בֵּית הַמִּקְדָּשׁ, קִנְיָן אֶחָד.

תּוֹרָה מִנַּיִן, דִּכְתִיב: יְיָ קָנָנִי רֵאשִׁית דַּרְכּוֹ, קֶדֶם מִפְעָלָיו מֵאָז.

שָׁמַיִם וָאָרֶץ מִנַּיִן, דִּכְתִיב: כֹּה אָמַר יְיָ, הַשָּׁמַיִם כִּסְאִי וְהָאָרֶץ הֲדֹם רַגְלָי, אֵי זֶה בַיִת אֲשֶׁר תִּבְנוּ לִי וְאֵיזֶה מָקוֹם מְנוּחָתִי, וְאוֹמֵר: מָה רַבּוּ מַעֲשֶׂיךָ יְיָ, כֻּלָּם בְּחָכְמָה עָשִׂיתָ, מָלְאָה הָאָרֶץ קִנְיָנֶךָ.

אַבְרָהָם מִנַּיִן, דִּכְתִיב: וַיְבָרְכֵהוּ וַיֹּאמַר: בָּרוּךְ אַבְרָם לְאֵל עֶלְיוֹן, קֹנֵה שָׁמַיִם וָאָרֶץ.

יִשְׂרָאֵל מִנַּיִן, דִּכְתִיב: עַד יַעֲבֹר עַמְּךָ יְיָ, עַד יַעֲבֹר עַם זוּ קָנִיתָ, וְאוֹמֵר: לִקְדוֹשִׁים אֲשֶׁר בָּאָרֶץ הֵמָּה, וְאַדִּירֵי כָּל חֶפְצִי בָם.

בֵּית הַמִּקְדָּשׁ מִנַּיִן, דִּכְתִיב: מָכוֹן לְשִׁבְתְּךָ פָּעַלְתָּ יְיָ, מִקְדָּשׁ

---

tion—G-d is "seated" upon them, i.e., lowered and revealed through them.

Abraham. Abraham devoted his life to increasing awareness of G-d among all people. That he was able to do this even in a pre-Sinai world is testament to his complete oneness with G-d.

Abraham...acquirer of heaven and earth. Because Abraham familiarized the people of his generation with G-d's existence—thereby giving heaven and earth back to G-d, as it were (*Sotah* 4b)—G-d considered him a partner in the creation of the world. Abraham is therefore called, "acquirer of heaven and earth" (*Bereishit Rabbah* 43:7).

The verse thus demonstrates that Abraham himself was an "acquisi-

tion," a transparent conduit of Divine revelation.

The people of Israel. Even as the soul of the Jew descends into the physical world and acquires some physical dimension, it retains its essential being as an actual part of G-d.

To the holy people who are in the land. The first verse cited speaks of the Israelites who were still in the desert, removed from conventional physical life. The second verse emphasizes that even as people *in the land*, immersed in an earthly world, they remain *the holy people*.

Holy Temple. The fact that it is a physical edifice, constructed of physical materials, does not detract from its ability to house the Divine presence.

world. They are the following: Torah—one acquisition; heaven and earth—one acquisition; Abraham—one acquisition; the people of Israel—one acquisition; the Holy Temple—one acquisition.

How do we know this about Torah? For it is written: *G-d made me [the Torah] His acquisition prior to Creation, before His works in time of yore.*[27]

How do we know this about heaven and earth? For it is written: *Thus says G-d: The heaven is My throne, and the earth is My footstool; what house [then] can you build for Me and where is the place of My rest?*[28] It further says: *How manifold are Your works, O G-d! You have made them all with wisdom; the earth is filled with Your acquisitions.*[29]

How do we know this about Abraham? For it is written: *And he blessed him and said: Blessed be Abraham by G-d Most High, acquirer of heaven and earth.*[30]

How do we know this about the people of Israel? For it is written: *Until Your people pass over, O G-d, until this people You acquired pass over.*[31] It further says: *To the holy people who are in the land and the noble ones—in them is all My delight.*[32]

How do we know this about the Holy Temple? For it is written: *The place that You, O G-d, have made for Your abode; the Sanctuary which Your hands, O G-d, have established.*[33] It further says:

Torah. Even as the Heavenly and transcendent Torah descends and is applied to the physical and lowly aspects of creation, it retains its inherent status as Divine Wisdom. One need not shatter the Torah's physical façade, the language in which it is now concealed, in order to reveal its oneness with G-d.

Heaven and Earth. Even in their physical manifestation, heaven and earth possess elements that point to a supernatural G-d, e.g., the fact that the sun and the moon do not grow old before us—a reflection of G-d's infinity—and the fact that the earth produces "something from nothing," a reflection of G-d's infinite power to create.

The heaven is My throne. Heaven and earth are called an acquisition because they are a conduit for Divine revela-

---

27. Proverbs 8:22.   28. Isaiah 66:1.   29. Psalms 104:24.   30. Genesis 14:19.   31. Exodus 15:126.   32. Psalms 16:3.   33. Exodus 15:17.

אֲדֹנָי כּוֹנְנוּ יָדֶיךָ, וְאוֹמֵר: וַיְבִיאֵם אֶל גְּבוּל קָדְשׁוֹ, הַר זֶה קָנְתָה יְמִינוֹ.

יא. כָּל מַה שֶּׁבָּרָא הַקָּדוֹשׁ בָּרוּךְ הוּא בְּעוֹלָמוֹ, לֹא בְרָאוֹ אֶלָּא לִכְבוֹדוֹ, שֶׁנֶּאֱמַר: כֹּל הַנִּקְרָא בִשְׁמִי וְלִכְבוֹדִי, בְּרָאתִיו יְצַרְתִּיו אַף עֲשִׂיתִיו. וְאוֹמֵר: יְיָ יִמְלֹךְ לְעֹלָם וָעֶד.

___

רַבִּי חֲנַנְיָא בֶּן עֲקַשְׁיָא אוֹמֵר: רָצָה הַקָּדוֹשׁ בָּרוּךְ הוּא לְזַכּוֹת אֶת יִשְׂרָאֵל, לְפִיכָךְ הִרְבָּה לָהֶם תּוֹרָה וּמִצְוֹת, שֶׁנֶּאֱמַר: יְיָ חָפֵץ לְמַעַן צִדְקוֹ, יַגְדִּיל תּוֹרָה וְיַאְדִּיר.

___

four stages of creation: *Emanation, Creation, Formation,* and *Actuality.*

[The first three worlds are completely spiritual worlds, each one progressively more self-aware and further from absolute Divine consciousness. The lower aspect of the fourth world, *Actuality,* is the physical world we inhabit.]

The thought that all of these worlds came into being for the sake of the fulfillment of Torah should inspire a person to serve G-d in the most perfect way, to implement the teachings of *Pirkei Avot*: going beyond the letter of the law (*Biurim*).

G-d shall reign forever.... This refers to the Messianic era when G-d's presence and glory will be fully revealed (*Midrash Shmuel*) and the purpose of every being will be fully recognized (*Tiferet Yisrael*).

___

RABBI CHANAYA BEN AKASHYA
To make Israel meritorious. An al-

ternative translation: G-d gave them much Torah and *mitzvot* to *refine* and *purify* them.

One would expect the Torah to reflect the oneness of its Author. Why then does the Torah contain so many different elements? Why are the *mitzvot* so varied and detailed?

Because G-d wished to refine the human being. And since the human being possesses many facets, the Torah and its precepts are multifaceted as well. Each aspect of the human mind and deed can be refined by another aspect of Torah (*Mikveh Yisrael; Biurim*).

Additionally, a person is transformed by his deeds. Thus the more *mitzvot* he actually performs the greater the transformation of his character (*Chinuch* 16).

[See further commentary on this passage at the conclusion of Chapter One.]

And He brought them to the province of His holiness, the mountain that His right hand has acquired.[34]

11. All that the Holy One, blessed be He, created in His world, He created solely for [the revelation of] His glory, as it says: *All that is called by My Name, indeed, it is for My glory that I have created it, formed it, and made it.*[35] It further says: *G-d shall reign forever and ever.*[36]

Rabbi Chananyah ben Akashya said: The Holy One, blessed be He, wished to make Israel meritorious. He therefore increased for them Torah and mitzvot, as it says: *G-d desired, for the sake of his [Israel's] righteousness, to make the Torah great and glorious.*[37] *(Makkot 3:16)*

The province of His holiness. This second verse emphasizes that the holiness of the Temple spreads to the Temple Mount (*the **mountain** that His right hand acquired*) and to the entire Land of Israel—*the **province** of His holiness* (*Biurim*; see *Ibn Ezra* ad loc.).

One acquisition. Each of these acquisitions reveals the presence of the *One* G-d (*Ohr Hatorah, Bamidbar* 198).

11. This *beraita* emphasizes the importance of every thing and every occurrence. Everything comes into being because G-d creates it and everything that occurs does so only because G-d causes it to happen. The very fact that G-d Himself chooses to create something or to cause an event to occur grants immeasurable importance and meaning to that thing or occurrence. In addition, G-d grants every being the ability to reveal His presence in this world.

To apply this idea practically: technological advances, for example, can and should be used to further reveal G-d's presence (*Biurim*).

● Since no two beings are alike, each one reveals the presence of G-d in a unique and inimitable way. It is thus the sum total of all the seemingly "small" revelations of Divinity caused by individuals all over the globe that will together bring about the complete revelation of Divinity, when *G-d will reign forever and ever* (see *Likkutei Sichot*, 25:334).

He created solely for His glory. Alternatively, for the sake of the Torah, which is called "glory" (see *Likkutei Torah, Acharei* 25d).

Called by My Name... Created... formed... made. These four expressions refer to the four "worlds," the

---

34. Psalms 78:54.   35. Isaiah 43:7.   36. Exodus 15:18.   37. Isaiah 42:21.

BIBLIOGRAPHY

BIBLIOGRAPHY

Abarbanel: Commentary on Avot called *Nachlat Avot* by Don Yitzchak Abarbanel. Constantinople, 1505.

Arizal (lit., "the lion of blessed memory"): acronym for R. Yitzchak Luria (1534-1572); universally accepted father of modern Kabbalistic thought.

Avodah Zarah: Talmudic tractate discussing the subject of idolatry.

Avodat Yisrael: Chasidic discourses on the Torah, festivals and Avot by R. Yisrael, the Maggid of Koznitz. Jozefow, 1848.

Avot d'Rabbi Natan: Commentary on Avot, by the Babylonian sage, Rabbi Natan, printed in all standard editions of the Talmud.

Baal Haturim: See *Tur*.

Baal Shem Tov: R. Yisrael, founder of Chasidism (1698-1760).

Bachaya: Commentary on Avot by Rabbeinu Bachaya ben Asher, student of the Rashba. Published from a British Museum manuscript in Jerusalem, 1970.

Bartenura: The primary commentary on the Mishnah by R. Ovadiah of Bartenura (1450–1510). First published in Venice, 1548. Subsequently appears in many editions.

Bava Kama: Talmudic tractate discussing the laws of torts and damages.

Beyond the Letter of the Law: Essays on Avot based on teachings of the Lubavitcher Rebbe by Rabbi Yanki Tauber. New York, 1995.

Binah L'itim: Discourses and eulogies by R. Azariya Figo. Venice, 1648.

Biurim: *Biurim L'pirkei Avot* by R. Eliyahu Friedman; a collection of the Lubavitcher Rebbe, R. Menachem M. Schneerson's comments on Pirkei Avot in often summarized form. First printed in 1982 in one volume and later published in two volumes in 1996 by Kehot Publication Society.

B'nyaot B'ramah: Commentary on Avot by Rabbi Shmuel Galanti. Lvov, 1801.

Brachot: Talmudic tractate discussing the laws of blessings and prayer.

Bereishit Rabbah: Genesis section of major collection of homilies and commentaries on the Torah, attributed to Rabbi Oshaya Rabbah (circa. 3rd century); some claim it to be from the early Gaonic period.

Chasdei Avot: Commentary on Avot by Rabbi Chaim Yosef Dovid Azulai (Chida). Munkach, 1834; Lvov, 1816.

Chasdei Avot (BIC): Commentary on Avot by Rabbi Yosef Chaim of Baghdad (known for his work *Ben Ish Chai*). Jerusalem, 1913.

Chatam Sofer: Responsa and commentary to the Talmud and Torah by R. Moshe Sofer of Pressburg (1762–1838).

Chida: Chida is an acronym for [Rabbi] Chaim Yosef Dovid Azulzai, who authored a number of commentaries on Avot: *Petach Einayim*, *Chasdei Avot* (above), and *Zeroa Yemin*.

Chinuch: Anonymous work on the 613 *mitzvot*, following their order in the Torah, believed to be authored by R. Aharon of Barcelona. Venice, 1523.

Chelek Yaakov: Commentary on Avot by Rabbi Yaakov ben Naftali Grinwald. Seinai, 1923.

Divrei Shaul: Commentary by R. Yosef Shaul Natansohn on the Torah, the Five *Megillot*, the Passover Haggadah and Talmudic Aggadah. Lemberg, c. 1877.

Eiruvin: Talmudic tractate discussing the laws of *eruv*.

Emet Mikotzk Titzmach: Collection of sayings by R. Menachem Mendel of Kotzk (1787–1859). Published under the name *Emet v'Emunah* in Jerusalem, 1940.

Etz Chaim: A compilation of the Arizal's Kabbalistic teachings, by his primary disciple and exponent, Rabbi Chaim Vital (1543–1620).

Etz Yosef: Commentary on the prayers by R. Chanoch Zundel ben R. Yosef, printed in *Siddur Otzar Hatefillot*. Vilna, 1928.

Gittin: Talmudic tractate discussing the laws of divorce.

Hatamim: Periodic journal issued by *Igud Talmidei Hatmimim*. Eight issues, Warsaw, 1935-1937. Reprinted in book form in Kfar Chabad, Israel, 1971; 1984.

Horiot: Talmudic tractate discussing the laws of one who disobeys certain rulings of the Jewish High Court of old.

Ibn Ezra: Commentary on the Torah by R. Avraham ibn Ezra. Naples, 1488; Constantinople, 1522.

Iggeret Hakodesh: Letters by R. Schneur Zalman of Liadi published as fourth section of *Tanya*.

Igrot Kodesh: Letters by R. Menachem M. Schneerson, the Lubavitcher Rebbe. 26 vol., Brooklyn NY, 1987-2003.

In the Paths of the Fathers: Commentaries of the Lubavitcher Rebbe on Avot, translated and summarized by Rabbi Eliyahu Touger. New York, 1994.

Jerusalem Talmud: See *Talmud*.

Kiddushin: Talmudic tractate discussing the laws of marriage.

Knesset Yisrael: Compilation of other commentaries and original commentary by Rabbi Yisrael Goldman. Satmar, 1924-30.

Kol Sofer: Commentary on the Mishnah by R. Chaim Sofer, Rabbi of Pest, Hungary. Munkacz, 1881-2.

Ktav Sofer: Commentary on the Torah by R. Avraham Shmuel Sofer of Pressburg (1815–1871), oldest son of R. Moshe Sofer, author of Chatam Sofer. Pressburg, 1889.

Kuzari: Important work on Jewish philosophy and theology, by R. Yehudah Halevi. Written as a dialogue between the king of the Khazars and a Jewish scholar. Originally in Arabic, translated into Hebrew by R. Yehudah ibn Tibbon. Constantinople, 1506.

Lechem Shamayim: Commentary on Avot by R. Yaakov Emden. Amsterdam, 1751.

Lechem Yehudah: Commentary on Avot by R. Yehudah bar Shmuel Lirma. Sabbioneta, 1554.

Lev Avot: Commentary on Avot by R. Shlomo bar Yitzchak Halevi. Salonika, 1565. Cited by *Midrash Shmuel*.

Likkutei Battar Likkutei: Anthology of other commentaries as well as some original commentary by Rabbi Shmuel Alter. New York, 1951.

Likkutei Sichot: Talks delivered and edited by R. Menachem M. Schneerson, the Lubavitcher Rebbe. 39 vol., Brooklyn NY, 1962-2001.

Likkutei Torah: A collection of discourses elucidating major themes of the weekly Torah portion and festivals according to Chasidic philosophy, Rabbi Schneur Zalman of Liadi. Zhitomir, 1848; Brooklyn, NY, 1965; 1999.

Maamarei Admur Hazaken: Chasidic Discourses by R. Schneur Zalman of Liadi. 24 vol., Brooklyn, NY, 1956-1995.

Magen Avot: Commentary on Avot based on Rashi, Rambam and Rabbeinu Yonah, as well as original commentary by Rabbi Shimon bar Tzemach Doran. Laverne, 1763.

Maggid of Mezrich: R. DovBer, disciple of R. Yisrael Baal Shem Tov, and second leader of the Chasidic Movement (d. 1772).

Maharal: Philosophic/mystic commentary on Avot called *Derech Chaim* by Rabbi Judah Loew of Prague. Krakow, 1589.

Maharam Shik: R. Moshe Shik (1807–1879), author of a commentary on Avot, among other works. A student of R. Moshe Sofer, author of Chatam Sofer, he established a yeshiva in Chust, Hungary.

Mefarshim: I.e., commentators. This term is sometimes used when the comment cited is not unique to any specific commentator.

Meiri: R. Menachem ben Shlomo, author of *Beit Habechirah*, an encyclopedic commentary on the Talmud that anthologizes many earlier commentators (1249-1316).

R. Matityahu Hayitzhari: Author of a commentary on Avot. Lived in the fourteenth and fifteenth centuries and was active in his hometown of Saragossa, the capital of the Aragon region of Spain.

Midrash Shmuel: Commentary on Avot by Rabbi Shmuel de Ozido. Arguably the most popular commentary on Avot to this day. It is an anthology of earlier commentaries—including Abarbanel, R. Moshe Almoshnino, R. Yosef Yaavetz (called 'HaChasid'), R. Moshe Alashkar, and others—as well as original interpretation by R. Shmuel de Ozido, a student of the famed Kabbalist, the Arizal. Venice, 1579.

Midrash Tanchuma: Early *Midrash* on the Torah, attributed to R. Tanchuma bar Abba. Constantinople, 1522.

R. Mendel of Kotzk: Famous Chasidic master (1787-1859), disciple of

Rabbi Yaakov Yitzchak (the Chozeh of Lublin) and R. Simcha Bunem of Pshischa.

Midrash David: Commentary on Avot by Rabbi David Hanagid, grandson of Rambam. Translated from Arabic with annotations by Rabbi BenTzion Krinpis. Jerusalem, 1944.

Mikveh Yisrael: Commentary on Avot by Rabbi Yisrael Prostiz-Shteinshneider. Pressburg, 1879.

Mili D'chasiduta: Compilation of commentaries that include the early commentators (Rambam, Meiri, etc.), Maharal, *Midrash Shmuel,* and the Chabad Masters by Rabbi Yekutiel Green. Kfar Chabad, 1997.

Mimayanot Hanetzach: Anthology of commentaries by Aharon Sorsky. Bnei Brak, 1979.

R. Moshe Alashkar: Spanish-born scholar, left Spain with the Expulsion in 1492, and later served as a judge in Cairo. Passed away in Jerusalem in 1542. Wrote halachic responsa printed in Sabbioneta, 1553.

Nachlat Avot: Commentary on Avot by Abarbanel.

Nedarim: Talmudic tractate discussing oaths.

Niddah: Talmudic tractate discussing the laws of family purity.

Notzer Chesed: A Kabbalistic/Chasidic commentary on Avot by Rabbi Yitzchak Yehudah Yechiel Sufrin of Kamarna. Lvov, 1856.

Ohr Hatorah: Chasidic discourses on Scripture by R. Menachem Mendel of Lubavitch, the Tzemach Tzedek. Berditchev, 1913; Brooklyn, NY, 1950 and on.

Ohr Samayach: Commentary on Rambam by R. Meir Simcha Hakohen of Dvinsk (1843–1926). First published during 1902–1910 in Warsaw and Riga.

Pesachim: Talmudic tractate discussing the Passover laws.

Petach Einyaim: Commentary on Avot by Rabbi Chaim Yosef Dovid Azulai (Chida). Munkach, 1834.

Pirkei Moshe: Commentary on Avot by R. Moshe Almoshnino. Salonika, 1563.

Pri Chaim: Commentary on Avot by R. Avraham Chaim, rabbi of Zlotchov. Lemberg, 1873.

Raavad: R. Avraham ben David of Posquires (1125-1198), author of generally critical glosses to Rambam's *Yad* and other works.

Ramah: R. Meir ben Todros Halevi Abulafia of Toledo, Spain (c. 1180-1245). Cited by *Midrash Shmuel*. Author of famous work entitled *Yad Ramah* on *Bava Batra*.

Rambam: Commentary on Avot by Rabbi Moshe ben Maimon (Maimonides). Constantinople, 1505.

Ramban: Rabbi Moshe ben Nachman (Nachmanides), Kabbalist and author (1194–1270). Composed numerous works, including a commentery on the Talmud, *Milchamot Hashem, Sefer Hagemul, Sefer Hageulah* and *Sefer Havikuach*.

Rashi: Commentary on Avot by Rabbi Shlomo Yitzchaki. See, however, *Lechem Shamayim*, who asserts that the commentary on Avot attributed to Rashi cannot have been written by Rashi.

Ritva: Commentary on Avot by R. Yom Tov ben Avraham Ishbili (1248-1330), author of a major commentary on the Talmud. (According to some, the commentary on *Avot* is by one of his students. See *Midrash Shmuel*, introduction.)

Sanhedrin: Talmudic tractate discussing laws concerning the High Court of old in Jerusalem. Also contains a chapter on the future Messianic era.

Sfat Emet: Commentary on Avot by the Rebbe of Gur, Rabbi Yehudah Aryeh Leib (1847-1905). Pietrekov, 1944.

Sforno: Commentary on Avot by Italian scholar R. Ovadiah Sforno (c. 1470-1550), author of major commentary on the Chumash. Venice, 1567.

Shaar Maamarei Razal: Section of a compilation of the Arizal's Kabbalistic teachings, by his primary disciple and exponent, Rabbi Chaim Vital (1543–1620).

Shulchan Aruch Harav: Code of Jewish law by R. Schneur Zalman of Liadi. Shklov, 1814; Brooklyn, NY, 1960-8; 1999-2004.

Siddur Rav Amram Gaon: The oldest surviving prayer book, by R. Amram Gaon (d. c. 875 c.e.). First published in Warsaw, 1865.

Sotah: Talmudic tractate discussing the law of the suspected adulteress.

Taanit: Talmudic tractate discussing fast days.

Talmud: The embodiment of the Oral Law. Following the codification of the Mishnah by Rabbi Yehudah Hanassi, c. 150 c.e., later discussions, known as the Talmud, were redacted in two parts. The more popular Babylonian Talmud was compiled by Rav Ashi and Ravina (about the end of the 5th century, c.e.). The Jerusalem Talmud was compiled by Rabbi Yochanan bar Nappacha (about the end of the 3rd century, c.e.).

Tanya: Famous philosophical work by Rabbi Schneur Zalman of Liadi, in which the principles of Chabad are expounded. Also called *Likuttei Amarim.*

Tiferet Yisrael: Commentary on the Mishnah by Yisrael Lifschutz. Hanover–Danzig, 1830-1845.

Torat Chaim: A collection of discourses elucidating major themes of the Torah portions of Bereishit-Pekudei, by Rabbi DovBer of Lubavitch. Kopust, 1886; Brooklyn NY, 1974; 2003.

Tosfot: A dialectic commentary on the Talmud, generally printed opposite the commentary of Rashi, largely the product of Rashi's students and grandsons (circa. 1100-1171).

Tosfot Yom Tov: Important commentary on the Mishnah by Rabbi Yom Tov Lipmann Heller. Prague, 1614-17.

Tur: Two works by this name were authored by R. Yaakov ben Asher. One, a code of Jewish law—also called *Arba'a Turim*—was first published in Piove di Sacco, 1475. The other, a commentary on the Torah, first appeared in Constantinople, 1514.

R. Yaakov of Amshinov: R. Yaakov David Kalish (1803-1878), founder of the Amshinov Chasidic dynasty.

R. Yaakov Emden: Author of *Lechem Shamayim* on Avot as well other works including a Kabbalistic commentary on the Siddur (1697-1776).

HaChasid Yaavetz: Colloquial for Rabbi Yosef Yaavetz; thus cited by *Midrash Shmuel.* His commentary on Avot was printed in Adrianopoli, 1415; Warsaw, 1880.

Yalkut Hagershoni: Commentary on Avot by Rabbi Gershon Stern. Paks, 1906.

Yevamot: Talmudic tractate discussing levirate marriage.

R.Y. ben Shlomo: Commentary on Avot by Rabbi Yitzchak bar Shlomo of Toledo. Published from manuscript in Jerusalem, 1968. Cited often by *Midrash Shmuel.*

R.Y. ben Shushan: Commentary on Avot by Rabbi Yosef ben Shushan, published from manuscript in Jerusalem, 1986. Cited often by *Midrash Shmuel.*

Yoma: Talmudic tractate primarily discussing the laws of Yom Kippur.

Rabbenu Yonah: R. Yonah ben Avraham Gerondi ("of Gerona"; d. 1263), teacher of the Rashba. Author of classic ethical works and a commentary on the Talmud.

Zechut Avot: Concise commentary on Avot by R. Yaakov ben R. Yosef Chaim of Baghdad. Published with *Chasdei Avot* by the author's son in Jerusalem.

Zeroa Yemin: See *Chida.*

Zohar (lit. "radiance"): basic work of kabbalah; compiled by Rabbi Shimon Bar Yochai (2nd century Mishnaic sage); written in Hebrew and Aramaic as a commentary on the Torah.

הוצאת ספרים

קרני הוד תורה

לויבאוויטש

MW00607891